The Pyramids Variatic

R A Chappell

How to use this book

The material in this volume is divided into three parts.

Part One presents an eight-module build-up to the Pyramids Concert Performance. Practically all pupils will be able to play the Concert Performance if they learn in the ways suggested, and it is not necessary to read music to do so.

'Build-ups' are an important element of the Musicarta approach. Practice sessions should review elements already learnt and revise features from simpler to more complex. Sample build-ups are suggested in Part Two of this book.

Teachers using the Pyramids Variations as lesson material can learn the music and the theoretical content of the modules and use the text as a 'script' to teach by demonstration and explanation. The teacher can decide on an individual basis how much of the theoretical background to present to the pupil.

Part Two contains 'performance prompts' and other memorisation aids to help the pupil play Pyramids without the music. Classically trained pianists often envy the popular music keyboard player's ability to play music from chord symbols or a lead sheet and playing from written music inhibits the development of this ability. Additionally, improvisation on a chord sequence is impossible without the chord sequence being properly memorised.

Part Three is a collection of variations which explore the musical potential of the Pyramids chord sequence through textural, melodic, rhythmic and harmonic variation. Playing these variations gives the pupil hands-on experience of what the improvising musician actually does and insight into the theory behind the improviser's creative freedom.

Preparing to Learn

Your purchase of the Pyramids Variations entitles you to a free download of audio-visual learning support material. To claim your download voucher, email your proof-of-purchase to webmaster@musicarta.com.

Once you have downloaded, organise your resources for efficient learning. A little time spent in advance of starting will pay off in multiples over your course of study. Tick the checklist boxes as you prepare to start studying the modules.

Audio, MIDI and video support files

Nearly every musical example in the Pyramids Variations comes with audio and MIDI support, so you can hear-and-see what to play without having to read music – and develop your ability to 'see the music in the keyboard'.

Your audio and MIDI files are in folders called PYRAMIDS AUDIO 1 to 4, PYRAMIDS MIDI 1 and 2, and PYRAMIDS VIDEO. Leave these files in these folders!

    ☐ Make a master Pyramids Variations folder on your computer.

    ☐ Put the support file folders in your master Pyramids Variations folder or other preferred location.

When you work on the Pyramids Variations, you will have the support file folders you need open to find and play the files easily. The folders you will need are shown in a table at the start of the module:

AUDIO 1	MIDI 1

The relevant support files are named in the table you will find closest to the example:

Pyramids_L1_A1	Pyramids_L1_M1

- The eight lessons which build up to the Concert Performance are designated L1 to L8. The Variations in Part Three are abbreviated – DBL for Developing the Bass Line, for example.

- 'A' designates audio (MP3) files; M designates MIDI files. If there is a video for the example, it is indicated with a V. Example:

Pyramids_L1_A1/V1	Pyramids_L1_M1

The audio files are MP3-encoded. Most media players will play MP3 files. Usually, you can just double-click the file icon in the folder to cue playback.

The video files are MP4-encoded. Double-clicking the file icon will usually cue playback. Your operating system will allow you to specify which application opens MP4 files. 'Splash Lite' is a good, free MP4 video player.

Introducing MidiPiano

MIDI files are computer-code music files. They can be played in many computer music applications. (Your computer media player will probably be able to play them as very basic audio files.)

To take full advantage of these MIDI files, Musicarta strongly recommends that you install and learn to use the free MidiPiano 'virtual keyboard' included in your support-material download. MidiPiano is simple to use, and shows the music in the MIDI file being performed on a virtual piano keyboard and scrolling past in a 'piano roll' pane as it plays.

This is a great help in learning and practicing your Canon performances. Musicarta strongly recommends you take the time to install and learn to use MidiPiano. Full instructions and alternative MidiPiano download locations can be found on the Musicarta 'MidiPiano' web page on www.musicarta.com.

MidiPiano is a Windows application. There are free virtual pianos for all platforms available on the Internet – 'Synthesia' is a good Mac/Linux-compatible alternative. If you already have sequencing software like Sonar or Cubase, you can use it to play MIDI files, but MidiPiano, with its many features and intuitive piano roll display, is recommended.

☐ Learn to operate MidiPiano or Synthesia.

Other resources

You do not need to be able to read music to start working through the Pyramids Variations. There are enough illustrations and other resources (like the MidiPiano performances and the audio files and videos) to ensure that you make good progress.

If you haven't worked from written music before, you will find the collection of flashcards included in the Pyramids Variations support download helpful. These cover the naming of the piano keys and the basics of written music.

☐ Print a set of the flashcards and have them at hand for easy reference.

Musicarta's 'MisterMusicarta' YouTube channel hosts Pyramids Variations material and there are also many resources at the main [www.musicarta.com] site to support your learning and encourage keyboard creativity in all its aspects.

☐ Bookmark http://www.musicarta.com and the 'MisterMusicarta' YouTube channel in your internet browser favourites.

Part One: Build-up to the Concert Performance

The Basic Music-making Position

The Basic Music-making Position

Musicarta's Pyramids Variations makes extensive use of the Basic Music-making Position (BMP). The Basic Music-making Position makes finding chords at the piano easy. It's a hand position where all the notes go together, because they are all notes of the same chord.

To start finding chords at your keyboard, copy the diagram below.

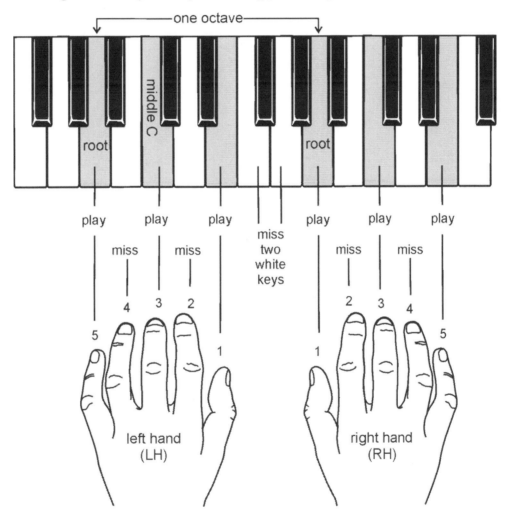

Each hand covers five white keys, with two unused white keys between the hands. You play the notes under fingers 1, 3 and 5 of each hand, and miss out the notes under fingers 2 and 4 (play one, miss one, play one, miss one, play one).

The two unused keys between the two hands ensure that the right hand notes sound good with the left hand notes, because the hands are 'an octave apart' – the bottom note in each hand has the same name (see diagram).

Naming and writing the BMP chords

Three-note Basic Music-making Position chords like these are named after their lowest (left-most) note. This name-note is called the 'root' (see illustration).

In musical jargon, the hands are playing 'triads in root position'. All six notes can also be called 'chord tones' because they are all proper notes of the chord.

The hands in the illustration are arranged to play an A minor chord. The lowest note of each chord – left hand little finger (LH5) and right hand thumb (RH1) – is an A.

In written music, with your left hand in the middle of the keyboard, these notes look like this:

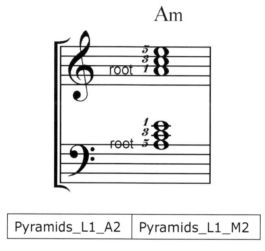

| Pyramids_L1_A2 | Pyramids_L1_M2 |

If you have copied the first illustration correctly, your chord will sound like the performance files in the table

The Pyramids chord sequence

If you look at the music example above, you will see the letters 'Am' above the written music notes. These letters are the 'chord symbol' for the chord "A minor". (That is how to say 'Am' out loud.)

Most popular music has a string of underlying chords called a 'chord sequence'. Good players of popular music read the chord symbols in the chord sequence to know which notes to play, often without using any written music at all. Learning Pyramids and using the Basic Music-making Position will teach you how to do this, too.

The following chart gives the chord sequence for Pyramids. You will play through the chord sequence, along the top line (bars 1 to 8), then along the bottom line (bars 9 to 16), using the Basic Music-making Position.

1							8	
Am ⇘	F ⇗	G ⇘	Em ⇗	F ⇗	Dm ⇗	E*	E*	⇗

9							16
Am ⇘	F ⇗	G ⇘	Em ⇗	F ⇘	E* ⇗	Am	Am

If, in the chord symbol, there is a small 'm' after the chord's letter-name, you say "minor" for it – "A minor" in bar 1, "E minor" in bar 4, and so on. Otherwise the chord is major and you call it by its letter-name alone. You don't have to say the 'major' part.

In the first versions of Pyramids, only Basic Music-making Position chords are used. The chord symbol names the lowest note in the BMP chord – the root of the chord – in both hands. So if you copy the Basic Music-making Position in the first illustration with your left hand little finger (LH5) and right hand thumb (RH1) on, say, 'F' notes, you will have found the six notes of the 'F' chord – bar 2 of the Pyramids chord sequence.

This way, you can play a whole piece just from the chord symbols in the chart.

E major and E minor chords

Pyramids is played on only the white piano keys, except for the E chord in bars 7, 8 and 14 of the chord sequence.

A Basic Music-making Position chord with LH5 and RH1 on note E, using only the white piano keys, produces a minor chord. But in bars 7, 8 and 14, there is no 'm' after the chord's letter-name E, so we know that a major chord is required.

To change the white-key E minor chord (Em) to an E major chord (E), we must raise the middle note from the white-key G to the key to the black G sharp (G©), just to the right of white key G (see illustration).

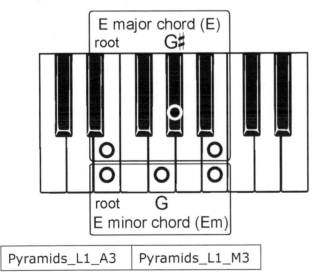

| Pyramids_L1_A3 | Pyramids_L1_M3 |

All the other chords, including the E minor (Em) chord, use only the white keys. You do not have to do anything special to make them major or minor.

Place your left hand little finger and right hand thumb on the name-notes, and let the Basic Music-making Position's 'play one, miss one, play one, miss one, play one' pattern find the chord for you.

The E major chords in the Pyramids chord sequence are marked with an asterisk (E*), but you will not normally get this helpful reminder.

The six-eight time signature

All music has a beat, or a rhythm, which is indicated by two numbers called the time signature. The rhythm of Pyramids is called 'six-eight'. You will find those two numbers on the left in this written-music example:

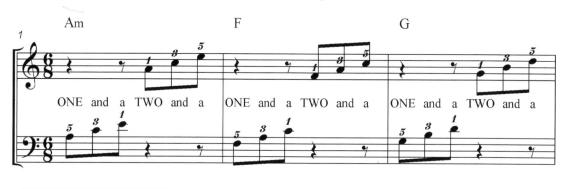

| Pyramids_L1_A4 | Pyramids_L1_M4 |

To get an idea of what 'six-eight time' feels like, play the performance files and say over and over to yourself:

"**ONE**–and–a TWO–and–a **ONE**–and–a TWO–and–a…"

…with each word coming as regularly as possible. 'One' is the strongest beat.

In this Pyramids Variations lesson, each chord symbol in the chord sequence stands for six evenly-spaced Basic Music-making Position notes, played from lowest to highest in the six-eight "ONE–and–a–TWO–and–a" rhythm.

The groups of six notes are separated by a bar line, as you can see in the music above. The written-music example also tells you which fingers play the notes. You can see that you play, in order:

- Left hand little finger (LH5), left hand middle finger (LH3), left hand thumb (LH1), then
- Right hand thumb (RH1), right hand middle finger (RH3), and right hand little finger (RH5).

This is the fingering of our Basic Music-making Position chords.

Playing the Pyramids chord sequence

Now you are ready to play the Pyramids chord sequence.

For each of the 16 chord symbols in the Pyramids chord sequence, you place your left hand little finger (LH5) and right hand thumb (RH1) on the name-note of the chord, as shown in the Basic Music-making Position illustration.

Then you play the six notes of the Basic Music-making Position evenly from lowest to highest (from left to right).

Here's the chord sequence again:

1						7	8
Am ↘	F ↗	G ↘	Em ↗	F ↗	Dm ↗	E*	E* ↗

9					14		16
Am ↘	F ↗	G ↘	Em ↗	F ↘	E* ↗	Am	Am

Pyramids_LI_A1	Pyramids_LI_M1

As you listen to the performance files, follow the music in the chord sequence chart.

The little arrows in the chord sequence show you whether the hands move up the keyboard (↗ – to the right) or down (↘ – to the left) to play the next chord. The first arrow tells you that, after you have played the six notes for the first bar (an A minor chord), you move your hands to the left (down) for the F chord, then up (to the right) for the G chord, and so on.

The asterisk on the E* chord symbol in bars 7, 8 and 14 is there to remind you to change the all-white-key E minor chord (Em) into an E major chord by using the black key G© (G sharp).

Practicing the Lesson performance

The written-out music showing the chord sequence being played using the BMP is on the next page. Follow in the music as you listen to the performances files again, then put it aside and try to play the chord sequence from the lesson instructions, without the music. Some illustrations you might find helpful are gathered together on the Lesson One Visual Prompt Sheet on page 70.

You might need some practice to get a smooth performance. You can improve your performance by playing any of the chords in the chord sequence over and over until you get six even notes.

Jumping to the next chord in a chord sequence without slowing down always takes practice. The secret is to let your left hand set off to find its new chord as soon as it has played its three notes.

It doesn't matter if your performance is a bit different from the written music or performance files as long as you find and play the chords somehow.

Pyramids: Chord sequence in the Basic Music-making Position

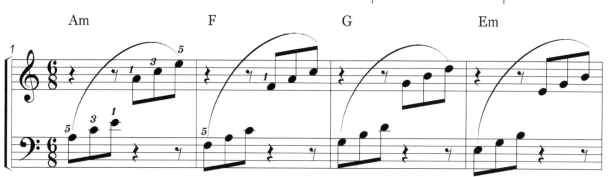

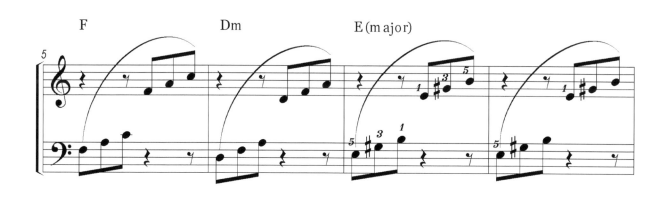

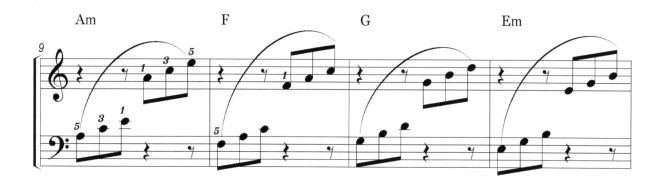

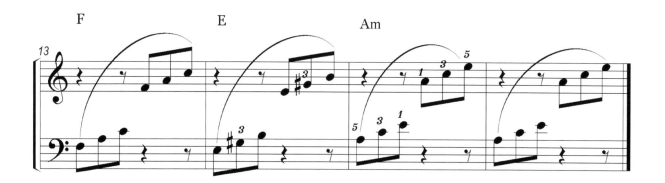

Left-hand-over Patterns

Looking at the Pyramids chord sequence, we can see two places where there are two bars on the same chord:

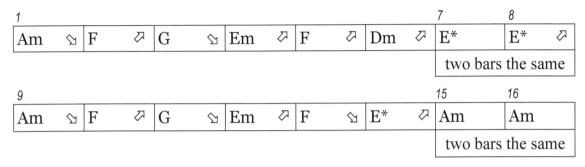

They are bars 7 and 8, on the E major chord, and bars 15 and 16, on A minor.

In these two places, instead of just playing the six Basic Music-making Position (BMP) notes twice from bottom to top, we can make a more interesting twelve-note pattern called the 'left-hand-over pattern'.

We are going to learn the left-hand-over pattern in our home chord of A minor. In the Lesson Performance we showcase it in an added-on Introduction.

The left-hand-over pattern

This is what two ordinary bars of A minor BMP notes look like in written-out music:

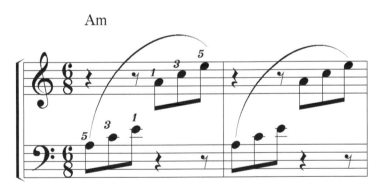

Pyramids_L2_A2 | Pyramids_L2_M2

In the left-hand-over pattern (which lasts the same amount of time) the left hand passes over the right hand to play just one note, and then you play back down again. Here's what that looks like in written music:

13

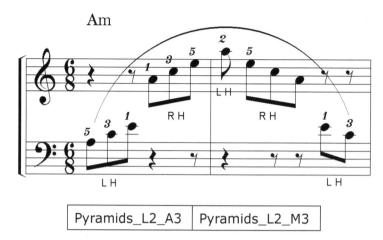

| Pyramids_L2_A3 | Pyramids_L2_M3 |

Here's an illustration showing how to find the left-hand-over note in A minor.

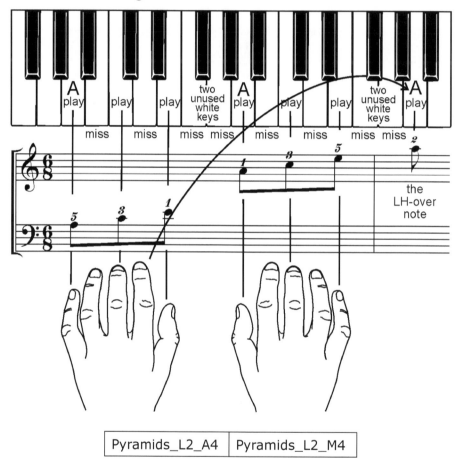

| Pyramids_L2_A4 | Pyramids_L2_M4 |

The left hand goes over the right hand to play the next 'A' going up the keyboard, then you play the notes back down again to fill up the bar.

In popular music, chords are our first priority. Along with the Basic Music-making Position, the LH-over pattern is one of the many useful chord shapes you will learn in the Pyramids Variations material...

We are going to play two LH-over patterns in A minor as an added-on Introduction to our improved Pyramids Variations performance.

The left-hand-over pattern introduction

Here is the Introduction written out, with instructions following:

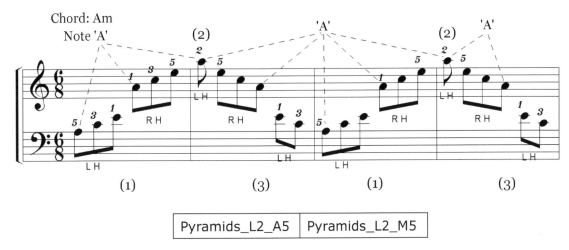

| Pyramids_L2_A5 | Pyramids_L2_M5 |

Read this 'walk-through' to make sure you understand LH-over patterns.

(1) First play the six A minor BMP notes from the bottom (LH5) to the top (RH5). This fills the first bar.

(2) For the first note of the next bar, bring the left hand over, leave two unused white keys and play the next 'A' key up.

(3) To fill the second bar, play downwards from the top RH note (RH5), just five of the regular A-minor BMP notes. Because the left-hand-over note takes up space in the second bar, the LH-over pattern ends on the middle left hand note.

Remember to leave two unused white keys on the way down when you're looking for where to put your left hand thumb.

Practice the pattern over and over. Notice any difficulties you have. Try to work out what your difficulty is and if any of the instructions or illustrations here can help you with it.

The left-hand-over pattern in E major

For bars 7 and 8, we need a LH-over pattern in E major. It's just the same 'shape' as the A-minor patterns above.

First play the six-note E major BMP pattern a few times to remind yourself of the notes to use. The middle finger of each hand (finger 3) plays the black key G sharp.

Here is a keyboard diagram showing the keys we use:

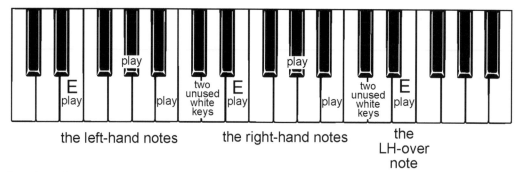

the left-hand notes   the right-hand notes   the LH-over note

Here is what the LH-over pattern in E major looks like in written-out music:

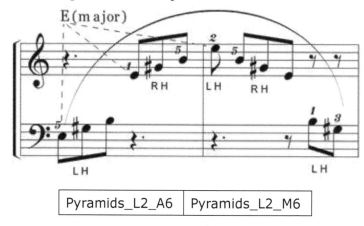

| Pyramids_L2_A6 | Pyramids_L2_M6 |

Follow the same instructions as before to play the LH-over pattern in E major.

(1) Play the six E major BMP notes going up.

(2) Bring your left hand over to play the LH-over note 'E'.

(3) Play five BMP notes downwards to fill the bar, leaving two unused white keys between your thumbs and finishing on the left hand G sharp.

Use the performance files to help you practice the LH-over pattern in E.

A left-hand-over ending

To finish, we want an A minor ending in bars 15 and 16 that uses the LH-over pattern. But if we play a full LH-over pattern, the last note will be C, the middle left hand note.

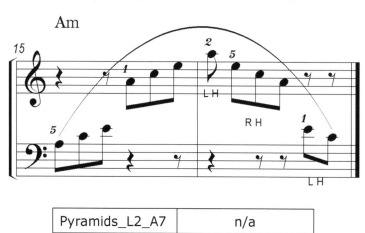

| Pyramids_L2_A7 | n/a |

This is not a satisfactory ending. Note 'A' is a better note to end on.

There are two possible A's we could finish on in the A minor LH-over pattern. The first is the LH-over 'A' at the top of the pattern:

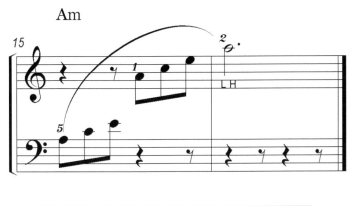

| Pyramids_L2_A8 | Pyramids_L2_M8 |

The other 'A' we could finish on is the RH thumb note, halfway back down the LH-over pattern:

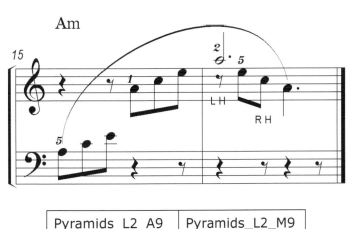

| Pyramids_L2_A9 | Pyramids_L2_M9 |

Try both of these endings. Neither of them is a full 12-note LH-over pattern.

The LH-over Performance chord chart

The new Pyramids performance uses the LH-over pattern in A minor, played twice, as an introduction.

Here is a 'walk-through' of the Pyramids with LH-over Patterns performance. As you read it, find the part of the chord sequence that is being described in the chord chart (below) and the Pyramids with LH-over Patterns music on page 19.

1. You play an introduction of two full A minor LH-over patterns. Remember that the last note of the Introduction is a C (left hand, middle finger).

2. Then you play six-note BMP patterns for six bars as shown in the chord sequence chart (exactly as for the Pyramids Chord Sequence in BMP music)

until you get to the two bars of E major at the end of the first half.

3. For bars 7 and 8, you play one LH-over pattern in E major (black note – G sharp). (Remember that the last note of this pattern is G sharp, the middle finger of the left hand.)

4. Go back to playing six-note BMP patterns for six bars as shown in the chord sequence chart.

5. For the last two bars you play the A minor LH-over ending you have chosen from the two alternatives given.

Listen to the performance files of the lesson performance and read through the list at the same time. Here is the new chord chart.

<u>Introduction</u>

Am	Am	Am	Am
LH-over pattern		LH-over pattern	

<u>Main Sequence</u>

_1_   _7_   _8_

Am ↘	F ↗	G ↘	Em ↗	F ↗	Dm ↗	E*	E* ↗
Ordinary six-note BMP patterns for six bars						LH-over pattern	

_9_   _15_   _16_

Am ↘	F ↗	G ↘	Em ↗	F ↘	E* ↗	Am	Am
Ordinary six-note BMP patterns for six bars						LH-over ending	

Pyramids_L2_A1	Pyramids_L2_M1

Your performance

Try to play this new LH-over version from the chord chart only. Only three small parts are different to the simple version you played at the end of Lesson One – the Introduction, the LH-over pattern in E and the LH-over ending in A minor.

Don't give up if you're not playing the music quite like it is in the audio clips. Use the combined Basic Music-making Position and left-hand-over patterns as a springboard to your own compositions. Remember that 'getting lost is the music' is part of the plan!

Pyramids with Left-hand-over Patterns

Adding the Melody

AUDIO 1 | MIDI 1   Lesson performance: Pyramids_L3_A1/V1 | Pyramids_L3_M1

Chords in a chord sequence on their own aren't enough to make a piece of music, or a song. We expect to hear a tune, or melody, as well, an in this lesson we add melody notes to the Basic Music-making Position (BMP) notes of the Pyramids chord sequence.

Here is a sketch of the new with-melody music. Use it help you understand the explanation on the next page.

Pyramids: Adding the Melody

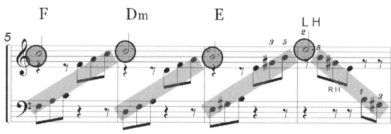

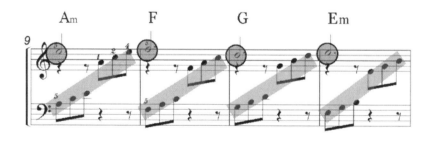

Pyramids_L3_A1 | Pyramids_L3_M1

There is only one new note in each bar – and all the notes from the previous versions are still there. The new melody note is in the most important position – the highest note, right at the start of the bar – so it is played at the same time as the lowest BMP note – the left hand little finger note (LH5).

Note that this very small 'sketch' music isn't meant to be played from. It's for you to look at in order to form an overall picture of the music in your mind's eye. The circles are the new melody notes; the rising slashes are the groups of six already-there BMP chord tones.

Check off the following five points against the sketch music:

1. There is only one new note in each bar.
2. This new melody note is in the most important position – at the top, right at the start of the bar.
3. The new melody is played at the same time as the lowest BMP note – the left hand little finger note (LH5).
4. The new melody note is always a BMP chord tone.
5. All the notes from the Pyramids with Left-hand-over Patterns are still there, but the Introduction has been dropped.

The numbered points above illustrate songwriting technique in general.

If chords come to you first when you're 'just messing about at the keyboard' promoting your top chord tones to melody status is an obvious but invaluable songwriting (or melody-writing) technique.

If tunes come to you first, this is still true. Your melody note – especially on strong beats like the first beat of the bar – will usually be the top chord tone of the supporting chord.

The melody notes added to a chord chart

Here are the new melody notes written into a chord chart above the chord symbols you already know.

	1			5				8
Melody:	E ↗	F ↘	D ↗	E ↘	C ↗	D ↘	B ↗	E (LH)
Chord:	Am ↘	F ↗	G ↘	Em ↗	F ↘	Dm ↗	E	E ↗

	9			13				16
Melody:	E ↗	F ↘	D ↗	E ↘	C ↘	B ↘	A ↗	A (LH)
Chord:	Am ↘	F ↗	G ↘	Em ↗	F ↘	E ↗	Am	Am

In bars 8 and 16 the LH-over note has been 'promoted' into the melody. Apart from those two bars, only the right hand plays the single notes in the 'Melody' rows in the chart, but both hands still play the six rising BMP notes indicated by the chord symbols in the 'Chord' rows. So the right hand now has a double job – melody notes and chord tones.

The little arrows in the chord chart show how the melody and the chord roots move either up (⬈) or down (⬊) when the chord changes. Notice that the melody and chord roots usually move in opposite directions. You will see this more clearly in the diagrams that follow.

Now, without trying to play the music, look at the music sketch again to see how both the music sketch and the chord chart show the same thing in different ways.

Learning the new version

The next example shows the new melody notes and the chord roots for the whole version, all squeezed into one line of music. (The LH-over notes are not shown.)

Learn these two zigzag lines of notes – there is a keyboard picture further on if you cannot read music. Use your index (pointing) fingers for all the notes, so that your hand moves from side to side, following the zigzag shape.

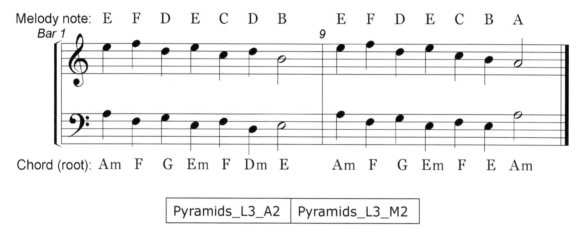

Melody note: E F D E C D B E F D E C B A

Bar 1 ... 9

Chord (root): Am F G Em F Dm E Am F G Em F E Am

Pyramids_L3_A2 | Pyramids_L3_M2

If we join the notes up and take away all the other lines, we can see the 'shape' of the music very clearly, and also how the two lines mainly move in opposite directions.

Melody note:

Chord root:

Try to play the little study above by looking just at this diagram instead of the music. Your starting notes are E in the right hand, and A in the left.

Now let's look at all we know about this new version in one diagram (next page).

You see the written music of the new melody notes and the chord roots at the centre of the diagram, the zigzag lines of the new melody notes (above) and the chord roots (below), and where to find the notes on the keyboard.

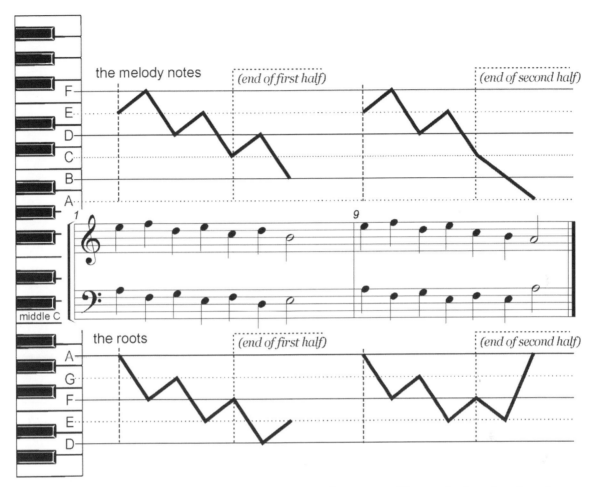

You might find you can copy the lesson performance files and already play the melody-added version from the instructions so far.

New fingering, and what the right hand actually plays

When we add the melody notes to the BMP notes, we find that it's better to play the right hand BMP notes with fingers 1, 2 and 4 so that we have the right hand little finger free to play the new melody note at the start of the next bar.

Here is a sample of what the right hand actually plays in this 'melody-added' version, with the new fingering given.

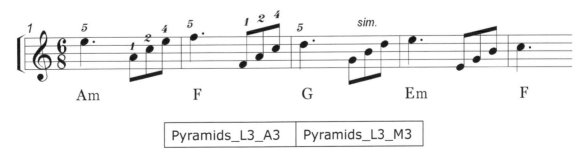

Here is what you are actually looking at in the music above:

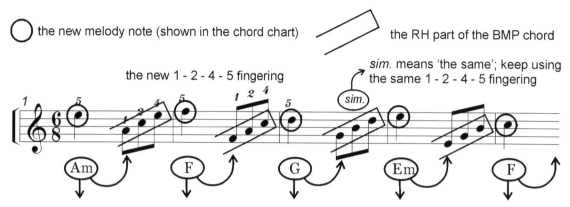

The first note in each bar is the new melody note. The other three notes in the bar are the right-hand BMP chord indicated by the chord symbols Am, F and so on.

Building up to your performance

Use the performance files and build up to your Pyramids: Adding the Melody' performance as follows

Build up to it as follows.

- Play the Lesson Two 'Pyramids: with LH-over patterns' version a few times.
- Remind yourself of the zigzag shape of the melody and the chord roots using the one-line study and the diagrams in this lesson.
- Add the new melody notes to the Lesson Two performance. You play these new melody notes with RH5 (the right-hand little finger) at the same time as LH5 (the left-hand little finger) starts playing the six BMP notes.

The music for 'Pyramids: Adding the Melody' (next page) is quite complicated to Try to play the new version without music first, using the performance files and the various diagrams in this module instead. Here is the chord chart with the melody notes added again, just as a reminder.

	1				5			8
Melody:	E ⤴	F ⤵	D ⤴	E ⤵	C ⤴	D ⤵	B ⤴	E (LH)
Chord:	Am ⤵	F ⤴	G ⤵	Em ⤴	F ⤵	Dm ⤴	E	E ⤴

	9				13			16
Melody:	E ⤴	F ⤵	D ⤴	E ⤵	C ⤵	B ⤵	A ⤴	A (LH)
Chord:	Am ⤵	F ⤴	G ⤵	Em ⤴	F ⤵	E ⤴	Am	Am

Try to make the right-hand notes slightly louder than the left-hand notes, so that the melody stands out. Imagining that your right hand is heavier than your left hand can help you do this.

Pyramids: Adding the Melody

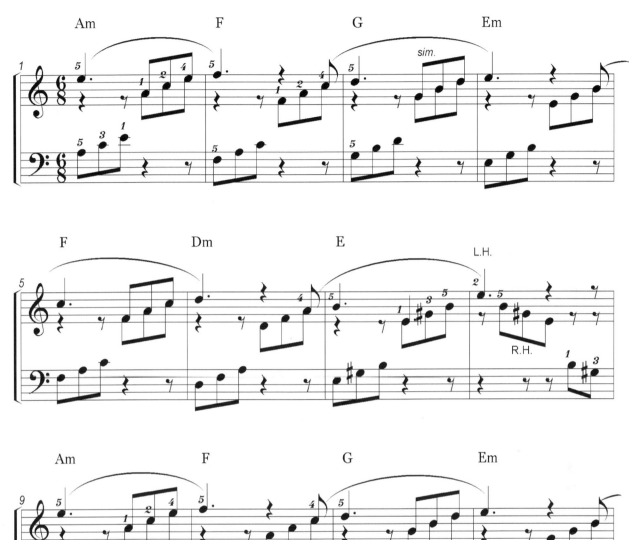

Lead sheets

Popular musicians often play music where only the melody and some chord symbols are given. Music like this is called a 'lead sheet' (pronounced 'leed') because it shows what the lead instrument is playing – the melody.

A lead sheet version of 'Pyramids: Adding the melody' might look like this:

Pyramids: Adding the Melody
(lead sheet version)

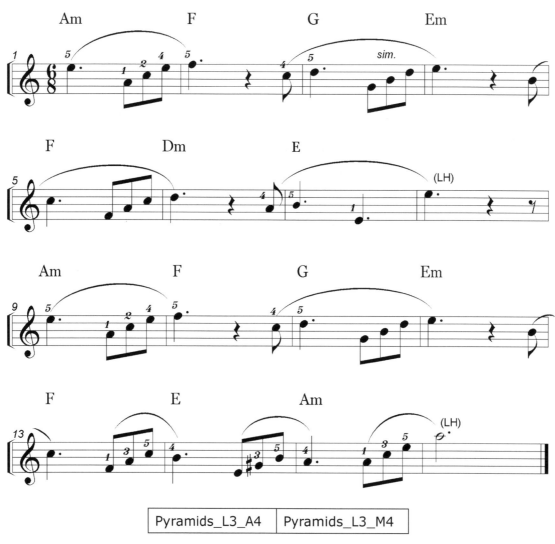

| Pyramids_L3_A4 | Pyramids_L3_M4 |

You see straight away that there is no piano accompaniment. There isn't even a stave (set of lines) for the left hand. Notice also that the stems don't all have to go up to make the melody stand out – there are no non-melody notes.

The only clue to the accompaniment is the chord symbols. If you know the Basic Music-making Position, you will be able to find chord tones which go with the melody.

Next, there is the time signature, which tells you what rhythm your accompaniment must fit into. The time signature is six-eight, counted:

"ONE–and–a TWO–and–a ONE–and–a TWO–and–a…"

There are six BMP notes, so playing them all will fill the bar.

Try playing the 'Adding the Melody' version from the lead sheet, making the melody notes shown in the lead sheet stand out.

The melody in the written music

Once you add a melody to the 'First Performance' music, the Basic Music-making Position notes become just 'the accompaniment'. In the 'Pyramids: Adding the melody' music, the stems of the melody notes all go up, but some of the right-hand BMP notes stems also go up – they have been 'promoted' into the melody. But all the right hand BMP notes – 'promoted' or not – still have their own (down) stems, to remind you where they come from.

In your performance, try to 'bring out the melody' by making it a little louder tyhan the rest of the notes,

Here are the first four bars of the full 'Pyramids: Adding the melody' written-out music, with a key to the things discussed.

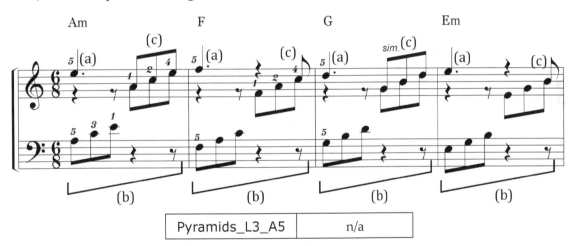

Pyramids_L3_A5	n/a

(a) These stems-up notes just after the bar line are the only new notes in the melody-added version. These are the 'Melody' notes in the chord chart.

(b) These bracketed groups of six (three left-hand, three right-hand) notes are the Basic Music-making Position notes you played in 'Pyramids: First Performance'. The chord symbol above each bar tells you how to find these notes quickly and easily.

(c) Notes with stems going up as well as down are BMP notes that have been 'promoted' into the melody. Try to play them with a little extra volume so that they stand out from the stems-down notes.

A Four-chord Version

| AUDIO 1 | MIDI 1 | Section performance: | Pyramids_L4_A1/V1 | Pyramids_L4_M1 |

Once you can locate Basic Music-making Position (BMP) chords on the keyboard using their name-note (root) – the lowest note in each hand – you can play a very grand-sounding version of Pyramids called the Four-chord Version.

In the Four-chord Version, you play four BMP chords for each chord symbol in the chord sequence. You start an octave lower than before, so that with the right hand now plays middle C. You play a left hand chord (1), a right hand chord (2), a left hand chord (3) and a right hand chord (4) all the way up the keyboard, like so:

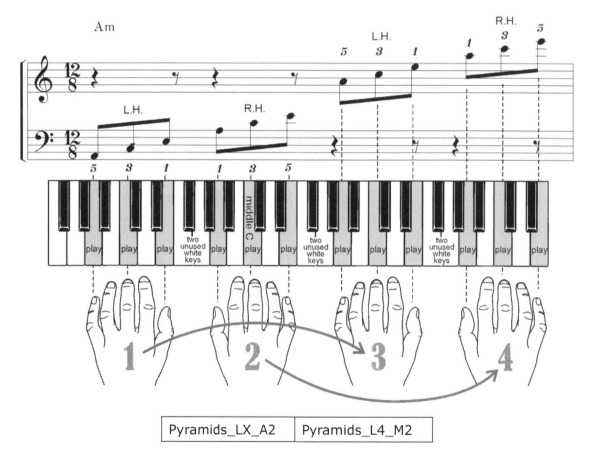

| Pyramids_LX_A2 | Pyramids_L4_M2 |

The twelve-eight time signature

If we are going to play four BMP chords for each chord symbol, there will be twelve notes instead of six in each bar. The time signature will have to be 'twelve-eight', with twelve quavers to the bar. Music in twelve-eight is counted:

"**ONE**-and-a TWO-and-a **THREE**-and-a FOUR-and-a…"

The notes in twelve-eight come at exactly the same speed as the notes in six-eight, so each bar is twice as long. They do not come twice as quickly just because there are twelve notes in a bar instead of six.

A sketch of the Four-chord Version

Let's look at a sketch of the Four-chord Version.

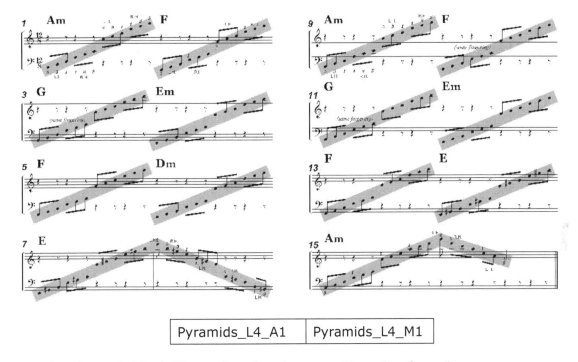

| Pyramids_L4_A1 | Pyramids_L4_M1 |

The 'sketch music' is deliberately printed too small to play from, but you can still see the chord symbols and the bar numbers. Listen to the performance files for this section, and get a clear picture of the Lesson performance in your mind's eye.

Pick out these features:

- The first half (bars 1 to 8) is on the first page; the second half (bars 9 to 16) is on the second page.

- For each chord symbol there is a rising groups of four BMP chords. These are the left hand, right hand, left hand, right hand chords played from bottom to top.

- You can see the up-and-down LH-over patterns in bars 7 and 8 (bottom line of the first page) and 15 and 16 (bottom line of the second page).

Try playing the first line of the Pyramids chord sequence using 12-note four-chord patterns.

1								7		8	
Am	↘	F	↗	G	↘	Em	↗	F	↗	Dm	↗	E*		E*	↗
Play four chords (LH,RH, LH, RH) for each chord symbol								Four-chord E major LH-over pattern			

Stop when you get to bar 7. We are going to look more closely at the double-length LH-over patterns next.

The four-chord LH-over patterns

Here is the full-size music of the double-length E major LH-over pattern in bars 7 and 8, at the end of the first half of the piece.

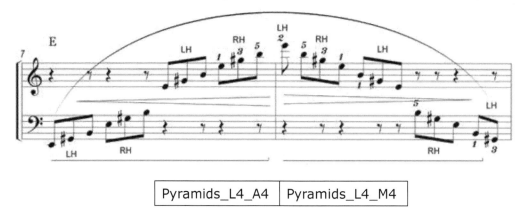

| Pyramids_L4_A4 | Pyramids_L4_M4 |

The E major LH-over pattern in bars 7 and 8 is made up of

1. Four chords going up. (You can tell these BMP chords by the beams joining the groups of three notes together.)
2. One LH-over note at the very top (E, the name-note of the chord)
3. Four chords coming back down, but...
4. ...only as far as the middle note of the last chord, to make up the twelve notes..

Add the four chord E major LH-over pattern to your first half four-chord performance, then play the second half of the chord sequence with four chords per chord symbol.

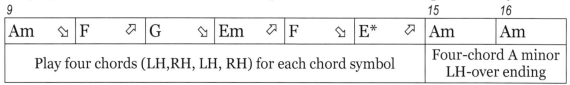

9								15	16
Am	⬂	F	⬀	G	⬂	Em	⬀	F	⬂	E*	⬀	Am	Am

Play four chords (LH,RH, LH, RH) for each chord symbol	Four-chord A minor LH-over ending

The ending, in bars 15 and 16, follows the same pattern, but ends either at the top or halfway down, as shown here:

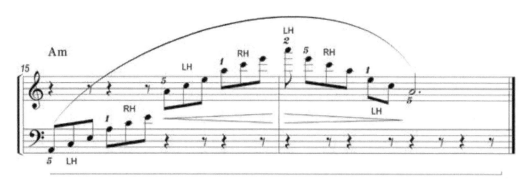

| Pyramids_L4_A5 | Pyramids_L4_M5 |

More helpful information is drawn together in the diagram on the next page.

The Pyramids chord sequence

The first half of the chord sequence					The 'end of the first half'		
1						7	8
Am ⬎	F ⬈	G ⬎	Em ⬈	F ⬎	Dm ⬈	E*	E* ⬈
six rising four-chord patterns						*up and down*	

The second half of the chord sequence					The 'end of the second half'		
9						15	16
Am ⬎	F ⬈	G ⬎	Em ⬈	F ⬎	E* ⬈	Am	Am
six rising four-chord patterns						*up and half-way down*	

Getting to the roots

Because the four rising BMP chords cover so much of the keyboard, it's quite a big jump back down to the start of the next four chords. It helps to be very sure of your target notes.

The notes arrowed at the bottom of the keyboard on the left (A, G, F, E and D) are the five notes (the roots) you have to get back down to from the last (highest) note of the previous chord.

The zigzag lines show the movement of the roots in the first and second halves of Pyramids. It is a good idea to rehearse this zigzag bass line – just these lowest roots – to help you remember where you are in the chords sequence and what your next target note is.

The A minor chord tones on the keyboard are shaded, including the very topmost LH-over note used in the ending.

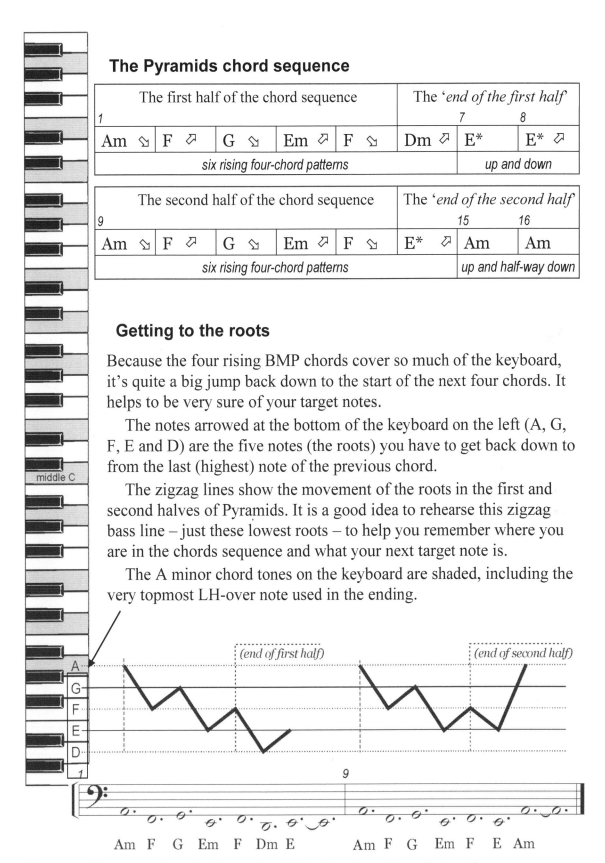

Now see if you can play the Four-chord Version from these instructions.

31

Pyramids: Four-chord Version

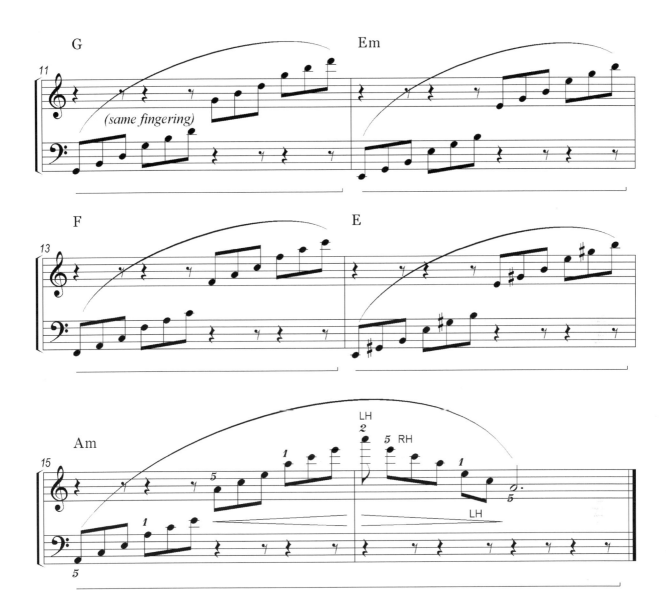

Pedalling

To make the four-chord version sound right, you need to use your piano or keyboard's 'sustain' pedal to keep important notes sounding that you can't keep held down with your fingers. In the Pyramids Four-chord Version, your main concern is to the roots of the chords – the very lowest notes – sounding.

The correct way to pedal is to push the pedal down just after you have played the first note you want to sustain. This is called 'pedalling up on the beat'. It's quite difficult to learn! One good way to practise good pedalling is to say out loud what you expect your right foot to do:

"UP down-a TWO-and-a THREE-and-a FOUR-and-a…"

Then you watch your foot to make sure it does what you're telling it to do. It's quite a fast off-and-on, but you will miss your bass note if your foot moves any slower.

Pedalling is indicated in music in several ways. Sometimes you will see ℘ and ✻ symbols to show when the pedal is to be depressed and released. Otherwise, you will find a line with either spikes or gaps in it, showing where to pedal.

It's easy to pedal too much and overwhelm your listeners and lose the music in the wash of sound. You must listen carefully to your pedalling and try to be 'tasteful'.

Playing the melody over the Four-chord Version

Section performance: Pyramids_L4_A6 Pyramids_L4_M6

The simple 16-bar Pyramids melody can be played right at the top of the four-chord Pyramids version. It sounds very impressive.

We start from the six-eight 'Pyramids: Adding the Melody' version. Everything in the right hand goes up an octave, and the left hand starts an octave lower. This leaves room for two more chords – the right hand and left hand chords 2 and 3 of the first illustration in this module.

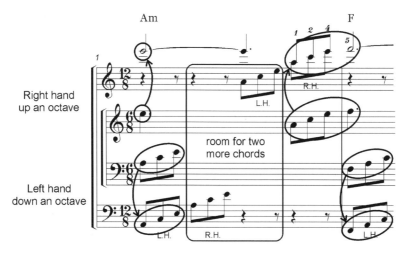

34

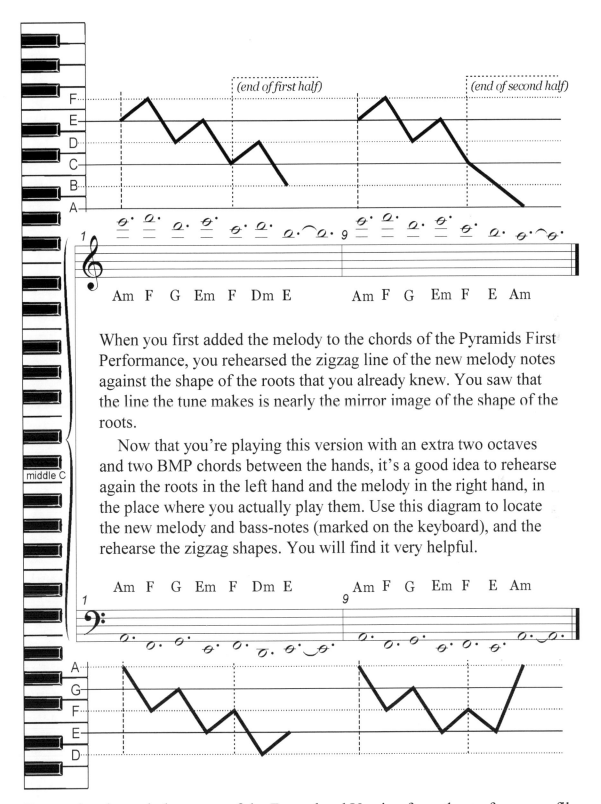

When you first added the melody to the chords of the Pyramids First Performance, you rehearsed the zigzag line of the new melody notes against the shape of the roots that you already knew. You saw that the line the tune makes is nearly the mirror image of the shape of the roots.

Now that you're playing this version with an extra two octaves and two BMP chords between the hands, it's a good idea to rehearse again the roots in the left hand and the melody in the right hand, in the place where you actually play them. Use this diagram to locate the new melody and bass-notes (marked on the keyboard), and the rehearse the zigzag shapes. You will find it very helpful.

Try to play the melody on top of the Four-chord Version from the performance files and instructions alone. You definitely need the sustain pedal to hold the melody and roots in this version. Listen carefully to make sure you pedal cleanly, letting all the old notes go and catching the important new ones.

Pyramids: Four-chord Version with Melody

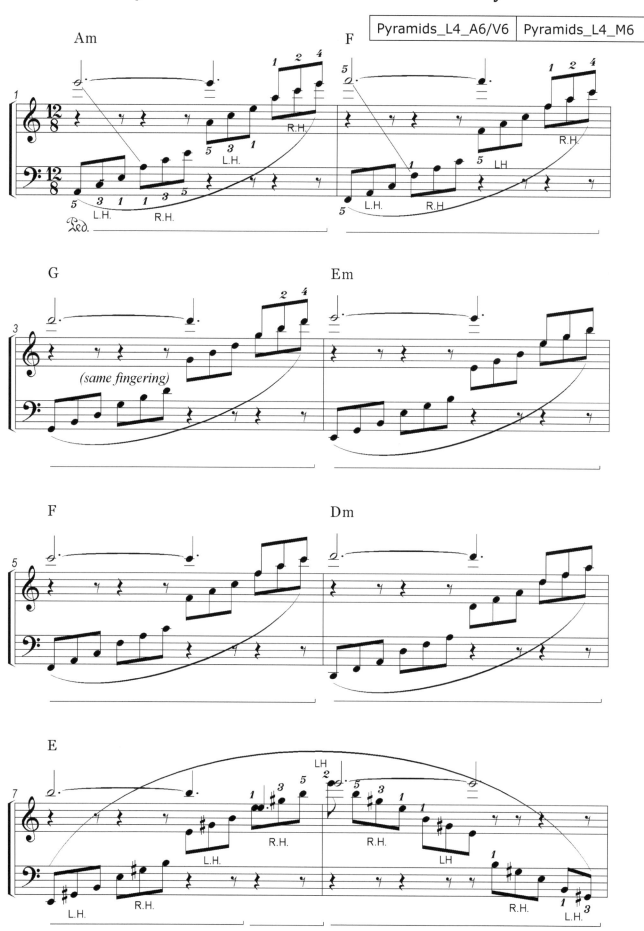

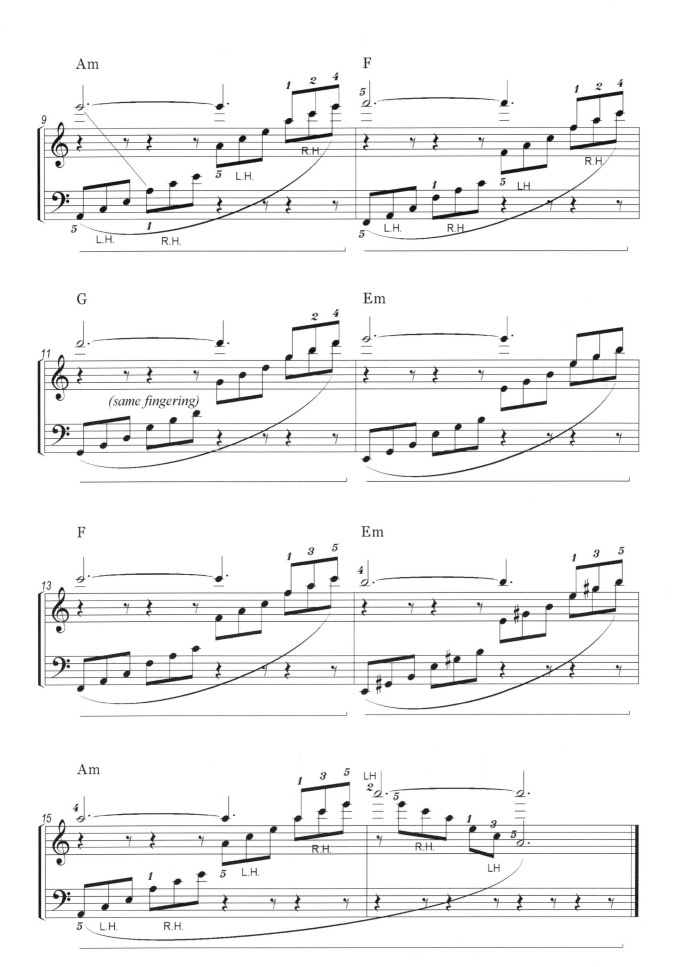

Developing the Melody

| AUDIO 1 | MIDI 1 | Section performance: | Pyramids_L5_A1/V1 | Pyramids_L5_M1 |

Chord tones are always first choice for melody notes, but in-between non-chord tones help give the Pyramids melody more character. Here's how the melody develops.

In Lesson One, the right hand plays only chord tones (BMP notes), using fingers 1, 3 and 5:

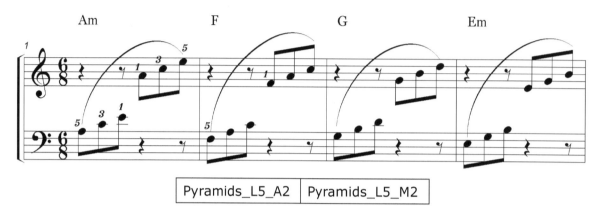

| Pyramids_L5_A2 | Pyramids_L5_M2 |

(Note: The performance files play all four musical examples in this section one after the other.)

In Lesson Three we added a melody note and changed the right hand fingering to 1, 2 and 4, to leave finger 5 for the melody note in the following bar:

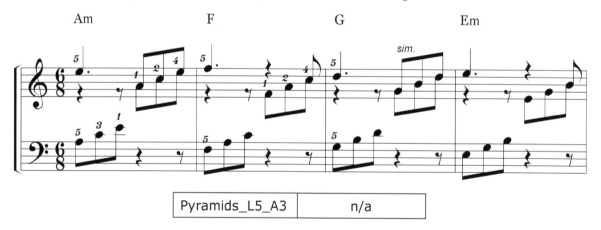

| Pyramids_L5_A3 | n/a |

"**ONE**–and–a–**TWO**–and–a **ONE**–and–a–**TWO**–and–a…"

In this lesson we are going to squeeze the note under the right hand third finger (RH3, arrowed) back into every other bar. (Note that you have to be using fingers 1, 2, and 4 for this to work.)

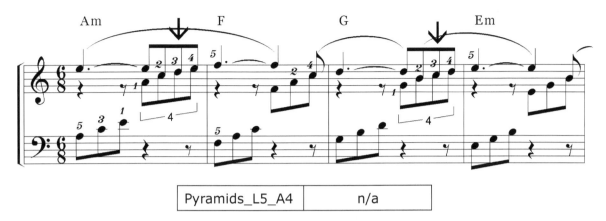

Pyramids_L5_A4 | n/a

However, it's difficult to play four equal quavers in the space of three, as shown in the music example directly above. So we keep the thumb (RH1) down for longer, and making the other three notes shorter:

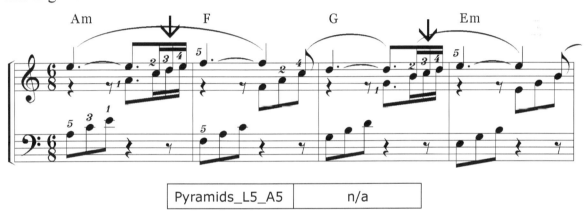

Pyramids_L5_A5 | n/a

The pattern of the developed melody

If you look at the first four bars of this developed melody, you will see that the first bar is 'fancy' (it has the extra note), the next one is 'plain', then fancy, then plain again.

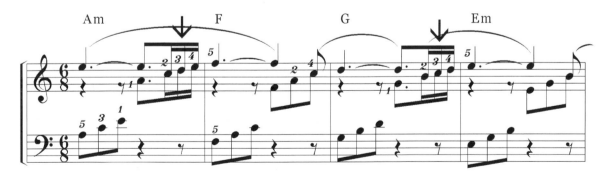

This fancy – plain – fancy – plain pattern continues for most of this new developed-melody version of Pyramids, as shown in the chord chart:

fancy	plain	fancy	plain	fancy	plain	(LH-over pattern)	
Am	F	G	Em	F	Dm	E	E

fancy	plain	fancy	plain	fancy	fancy	(LH-over ending)	
Am	F	G	Em	F	E	Am	Am

Always be on the look-out for patterns like this. It's so much easier to learn just two things - a 'fancy' and a 'plain' - and 'get' the overall pattern, than to read every note as it comes along.

If you understand the fancy/plain explanation, you can play most of the Pyramids developed-melody version using only this chord chart. Make sure you are using RH fingers 1, 2 and 4 for the BMP notes, and squeeze in the note under RH finger 3 in the 'fancy' bars.

The developed melody in bars 13 and 14

The only place the 'squeezing the third finger back in' technique won't work is in bars 13 and 14, where the melody falls instead of rising.

Here is the First Performance version of bars 13 through to the end:

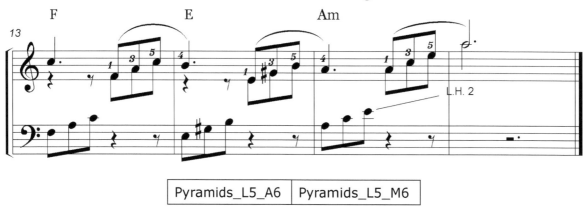

Pyramids_L5_A6	Pyramids_L5_M6

(Note: The performance file shows the whole process, as before.)

First, swap the order of fingers 3 and 5 in bars 13 and 14:

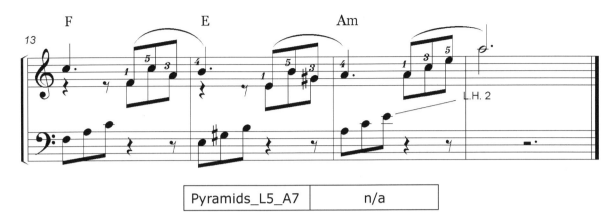

Pyramids_L5_A7	n/a

Then squeeze a **fourth finger** note in (arrowed):

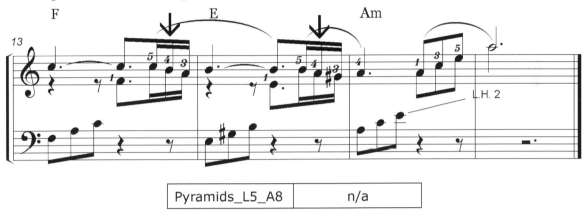

Pyramids_L5_A8	n/a

That explains all of the 'fancy' bars in the developed-melody chord chart.

Finally, we add a little decoration to the melody right at the beginning: This little decoration is known as a 'shake'. It's made up of the first melody note and the note below it, and you literally 'shake' your wrist to play it.

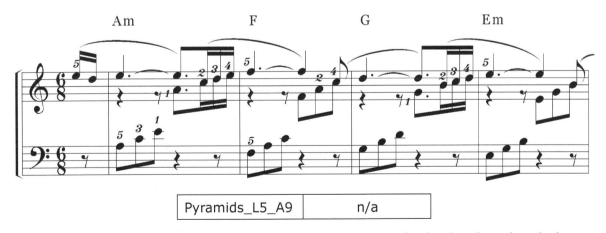

Pyramids_L5_A9	n/a

Now you have seen all of the developed-melody elements in the developed melody chord chart (above).

The music for the developed melody version is on page 43, but see if you can play a developed melody version just from these instructions. It doesn't matter if your version is a little different from the written music.

Or, try playing the developed-melody version from this lead sheet. As before (Lesson Three), you supply as many of the six bottom-to-top BMP notes indicated by the chord symbols as will fit, before you have to stop to play the melody notes.

Pyramids: Developing the Melody
(Lead sheet version)

Pyramids: Developing the Melody

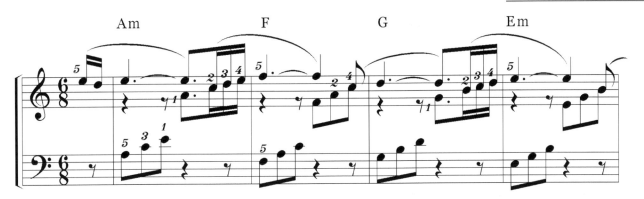

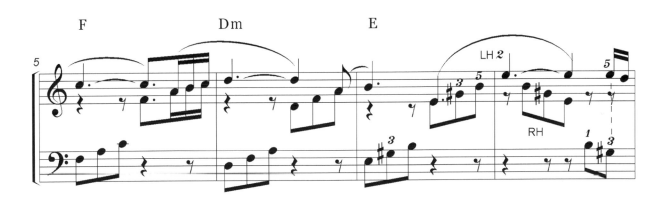

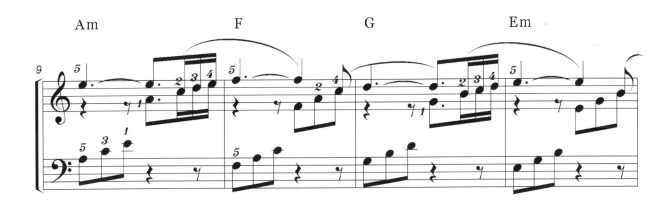

Playing the developed melody, four-chord version

Section performance: | Pyramids_L5_A10 | Pyramids_L5_M10 |

The next step is to play the developed melody over the four-chord base. To do this, you must already be able to play the 'Pyramids: Four-chord Version with Melody' (Lesson Four, Part Two) on page 36.

It's a good idea to 'build up' to a complicated performance like this. Using this chord chart to help you:

The first half of the chord sequence					The 'end of the first half'		
fancy	plain	fancy	plain	fancy	plain	7	8
Am ↘	F ↗	G ↘	Em ↗	F ↘	Dm ↗	E*	E* ↗
six rising four-chord patterns					LH-over pattern		

The second half of the chord sequence					The 'end of the second half'		
fancy	plain	fancy	plain	fancy	fancy	15	16
Am ↘	F ↗	G ↘	Em ↗	F ↘	E* ↗	Am	Am
six rising four-chord patterns					LH-over pattern		

- First, play just the Pyramids chord sequence (no melody) in twelve-eight, with four (LH, RH, LH, RH) BMP chords for each chord symbol (page 32).

  | Pyramids_L4_A1 | Pyramids_L4_M1 |

- Without stopping (if you can), repeat, playing the simple melody over the four-chord base. You have to use the sustain pedal to hold the roots and the melody notes. Try to 'bring out the melody' – including the 'promoted' notes (page 36).

  | Pyramids_L4_A6 | Pyramids_L4_M6 |

- Then play the chord sequence again with the developed melody, squeezing the third and fourth fingers back into the BMP chords according to the plain/fancy pattern.

  | Pyramids_L5_A10 | Pyramids_L5_M10 |

The written-out music for this developed melody, four-chord performance is shown on the next two pages. The music is complicated. It is easier and more profitable in the long run to build your performance from these instructions and your own understanding of what your going to do.

Pyramids: Developed Melody, Four-chord Version

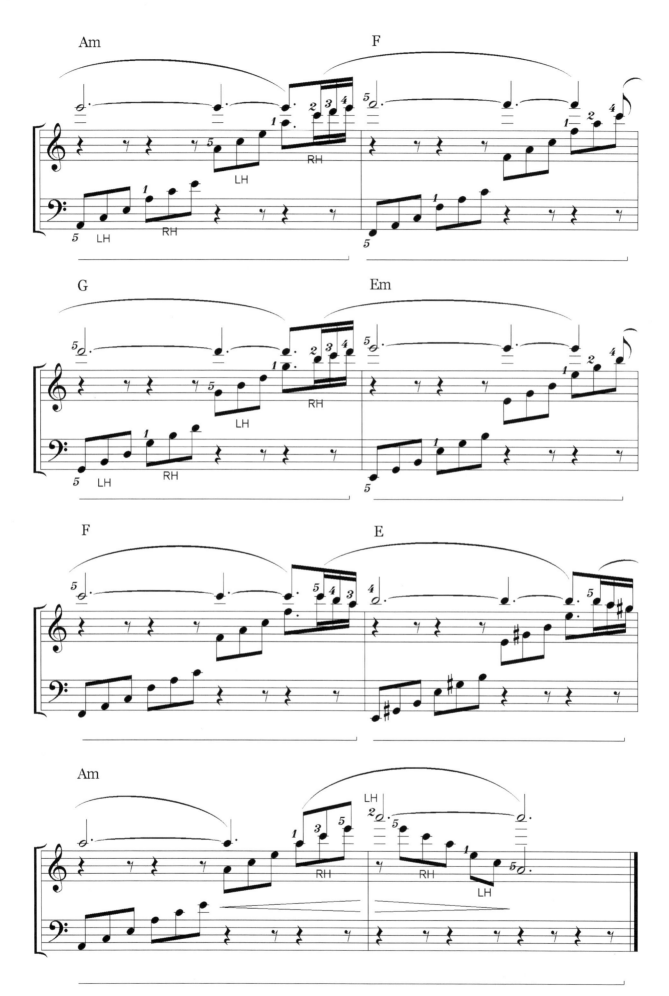

The 32-bar AABA Form

| AUDIO 1 | MIDI 1 | Lesson performance: | Pyramids_L6_A1/V6 | Pyramids_L6_M1 |

The Pyramids versions you have been playing up to now are quite short – only 16 bars long. To make the piece any longer without simply repeating the same music, we need a new, different, bit of music.

This new material is called 'the B section' – just why is explained further on. It will make up bars 17 to 24 of our extended piece, which we finish off with our usual last eight bars. This gives Pyramids its final 32-bar AABA form.

The 32-bar AABA chord progression is often used in popular song, especially the jazz standards of the 'Great American Songbook'.

The new music

Here is a sketch of the new music, made of the top (melody) and bottom (bass) notes. It's good practice to learn these lines before you add the chords in.

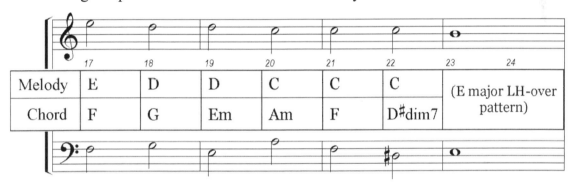

	17	18	19	20	21	22	23	24
Melody	E	D	D	C	C	C	(E major LH-over pattern)	
Chord	F	G	Em	Am	F	D#dim7		

| Pyramids_L6_A2 | Pyramids_L6_M2 |

Here is your zigzag line diagram of the same music:

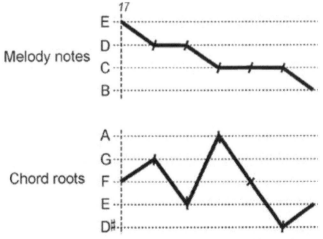

Make sure you can play the top and bottom lines from the line diagram, too.

Now add in the left hand chords only:

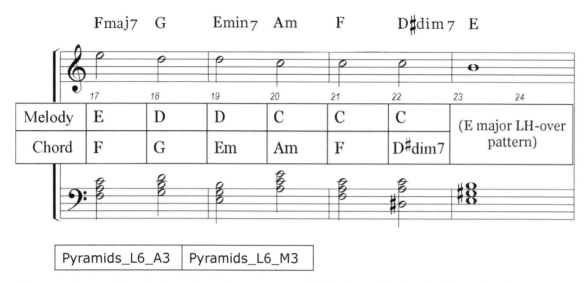

Pyramids_L6_A3 | Pyramids_L6_M3

You see immediately that there is one non-BMP chord in the left hand – the D sharp diminished chord in bar 22. It's explained in full further on in this module. You can read the left hand notes or copy from the keyboard diagram further down this page, or get them from the MIDI performance.

The right hand has to play chord tones as well as melody notes. If we add those right hand chord tones in, we get this diagram showing all the elements of the new 'B section' music.

Look at the numbered features:

1. The stems-up notes in the treble clef are the melody notes.

2. The stems-down notes in the treble clef are the right hand chord tones. Most of them are plain Basic Music-making Position (BMP) chords, in spite of the fancy chord names.

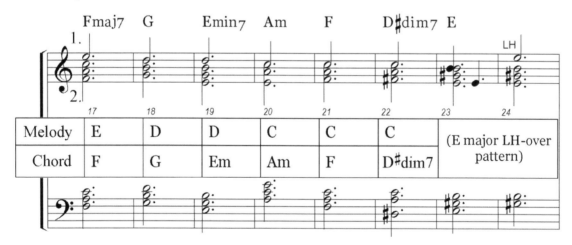

The new chords (Fmaj7, Emin7, D#dim7) are examined in detail one section further on, but first let's look at written-out six-note BMP patterns under the new melody notes, derived from the chord symbols in the 'Chord' row of the table.

The written-out B section music

The simplest B section music looks like this.

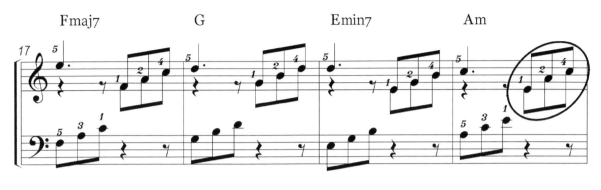

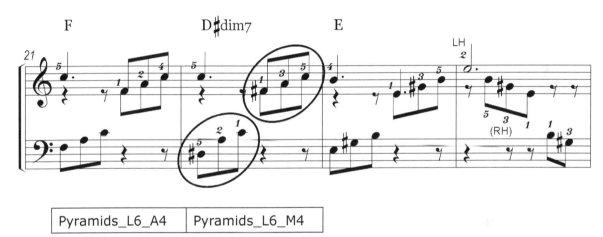

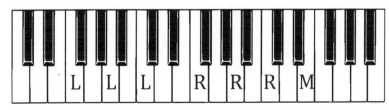

As before, our first impulse in a Pyramids performance is to play six rising BMP notes according to the chord symbol. Even the F major 7 and the E minor seven chords have these six simple notes. (They are only complex because the new melody note is not a BMP chord tone.)

The three-note chords which are not simple BMP chords are circled in the music above, and you can find these chords in the diagrams which come next. Otherwise, you can see that the pattern is the same as before: one melody note at the start of the bar, and six rising (left hand, right hand) BMP chord tones.

The new B section chords

You will notice that there are more complex chord symbols in the B section chord chart. Here are keyboard diagrams and audio/MIDI clips for the more complex chords.

The F major seventh chord (Fmaj7, bar 17)

49

(Key: L = LH note R = RH note M = melody note – also right hand)

Pyramids_L6_A5	Pyramids_L6_M5

(Note: The audio and MIDI files in the table play all four chords in this section one after the other in the order they are presented.)

The added note E, the seventh note above the root F, gives this chord its name.

The E minor seventh chord (Emin7, bar 19)

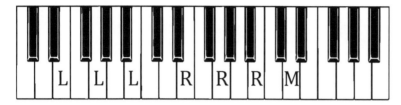

The added note D, the seventh note above the root E, gives this chord its name, but the chord is minor, hence 'minor seventh'.

The A minor (inversion) chord (bar 20)

Note that the hands share a note and the right hand is playing an **inversion** of the A minor BMP chord.

The D sharp diminished seventh chord (D#dim7, bar 22)

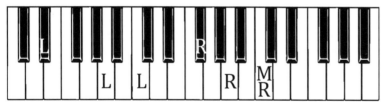

(Key: L = LH note R = RH note M = melody note)

The notes of a diminished chord are spaced a minor third apart – but you do not have to use all of them.

Expanding Pyramids to 32-bar AABA form

The two halves of the Pyramids 16-bar chord sequence are the same as far as bars 6 and 14. Music textbooks would describe it as having 'AA' form, or more precisely. 'A^{1}A^2' form, because the halves end slightly differently.

The new, different section of music needed to make the piece longer is called the 'B section'. 'A' and 'B' have nothing to do with the notes or chords A and B, but are only used to stand for eight-bar sections of music that are either the same (like A^1 and A^1) or nearly the same (A^1 and A^2), or different, like A and B.

We are going to make Pyramids twice as long by playing four 8-bar sections of the chord sequence in this order: A^1, A^1, B, A^2. This structure is usually just called "AABA form" – you say just the four letters names, without the little numbers.

In the new 32-bar Pyramids 'AABA' piece, the second 8-bar section really is the same as the first – otherwise the piece would end at bar 16. The slightly different eight-bar A^2 section is saved for the real ending.

Here is the full 32-bar chord sequence:

Pyramids 32-bar AABA form

A^1	1			same as first half of short version				(LH-over pattern)
	Am	F	G	Em	F	Dm	E	E

A^1	9			same as first half of short version				(LH-over pattern)
	Am	F	G	Em	F	Dm	E	E

B	17			new section				(LH-over pattern)
	Fmaj7	G	Em7	Am	F	D#dim7	E	E

A^2	25			same as second half of short version				(LH-over ending)
	Am	F	G	Em	F	E ⬈	Am	Am

If you can play the basic B section music from the instructions so far, you can slot it into the music you already know (rearranged) and play a 32-bar version of Pyramids. You play the first half of our familiar 16-bar version (A1) twice, the new (simple) B section music (page 49), and the second half of the 16-bar version (A2).

Developing the B section melody

The melody in the new B section now needs to be developed to match the developed melody in the rest of the piece. Just as in Lesson Five, we squeeze third or fourth fingers in to make little runs of notes.

Before you try to play it, study the written music use the bullet list below while you listen to the audio and/or watch the MIDI performance. (Both files play the music you see twice. Remember that you can slow the MIDI performance down.)

- The third finger is squeezed in bars 18, 20 and 21, going up.

- The fourth finger is squeezed in bar 22, coming down.

- There is a repeated melody note across the bar line three times (bars 18/19, 20/21 and 21/22). Use different fingers – RH4 and 5 – for the repeated note.

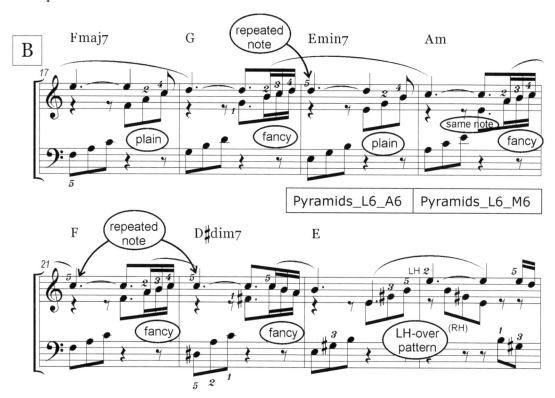

Pyramids_L6_A6 | Pyramids_L6_M6

- Watch for the thumbs playing the same note E in bar 20, where the right hand plays the second inversion A minor triad.

- Notice when the melody is 'fancy' and when it is 'plain'. The pattern is:

  plain □ fancy □ plain □ fancy □ fancy □ fancy □ LH-over pattern

The music for the Pyramids 32-bar AABA Form performance is printed on the following pages, but try to play the 32-bar Pyramids version from the more creative non-manuscript build-up in this lesson.

Learning the Pyramids 32-bar version

Here is a melody note/chord root zigzag line diagram for the full 32-bar Pyramids AABA version. Study it to get an overall view of the 32-bar form. It will help you 'keep you place' when playing the longer version.

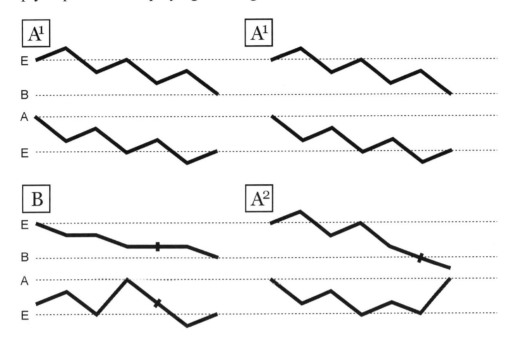

The AABA structure is often used in popular song, especially jazz standards. Listen out for AABA form in instrumental pieces and songs and look at the chord symbols in your sheet music for examples.

Pyramids: 32-bar AABA form

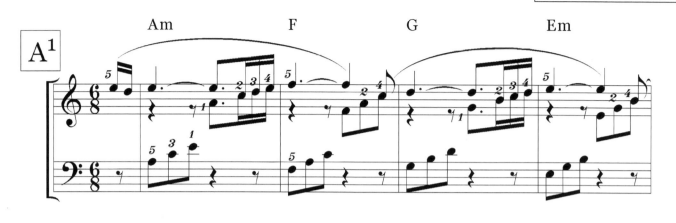

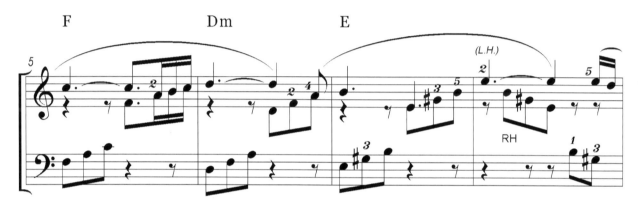

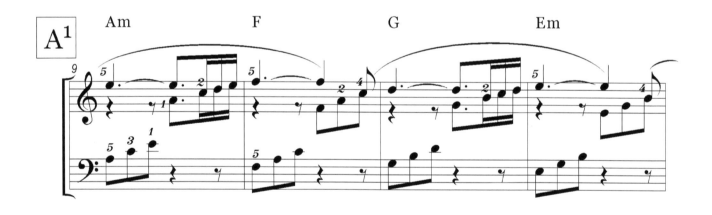

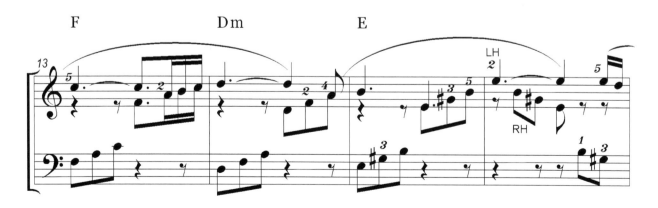

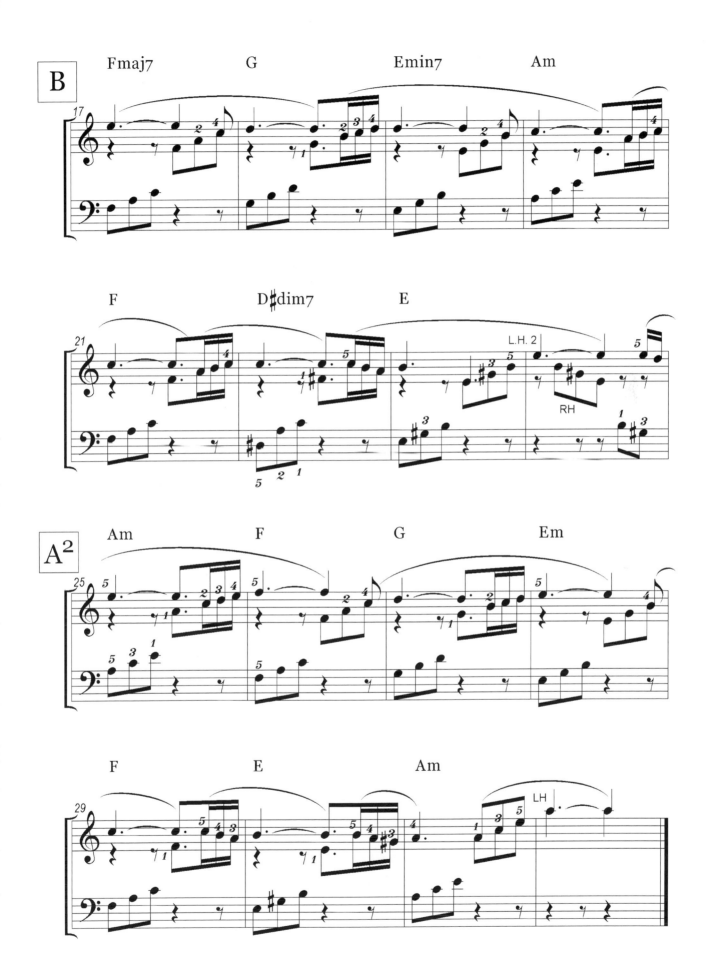

The Four-chord B Section

| AUDIO 1 | MIDI 1 | Lesson performance: | Pyramids_L7_A1/V1 | Pyramids_L7_M1 |

The four-chord AABA version of Pyramids is the basis of the Pyramids Concert Performance version we are working towards. The B section you learned in the previous lesson now needs to be expanded to a four-chord version.

Expanding the B section

To expand the two-chord B section, we use the same method that we used to create the four-chord versions of Pyramids, starting on page 28. We put the right hand up an octave and the left hand down, leaving room for two more chords in the middle. The bars become twice as long.

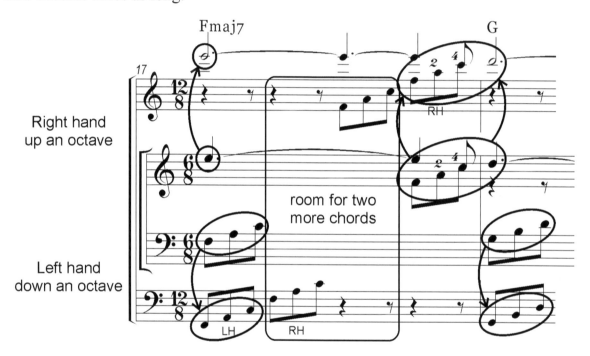

This method of expanding the two-chord version into a four-chord version works for the Fmaj7, G, Emin7 and F chords (bars 17, 18, 19 and 21)

17			20		22		23 (LH-over pattern)	
Fmaj7	G	Em7	Am	F	D♯dim7	E	E

Note that:

- Even though the Fmaj7 and Emin7 chords have more complicated names, the hands still play basic root position triads (BMP chords). It is the new melody note which makes the chord symbol more complicated.

- You have already played F, G and E minor four-chord patterns in the previous four-chord versions.

- Bars 23 and 24 are a left-hand-over pattern, which you have also played already.

That covers six bars of the B section, leaving only the Am (A minor) and D#dim7 bars.

The four-chord A minor pattern (bar 20)

The two-chord A minor pattern in the B section of previous versions of Pyramids has an 'overlap' – both thumbs use the E above middle C. (This is to stop the chords climbing higher than the melody note, C, at the top.) The four-chord version of this bar has the overlap in exactly the same place. To make the four-chord version, you play identical left and right hand chords either side of the original pair:

| Pyramids_L7_A2 | Pyramids_L7_M2 |

Here are the A minor keys shown on the keyboard. Only the chord tones are shown – not all the 'developed melody' notes.

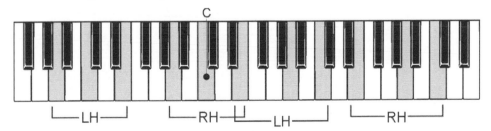

The two highest chords are inversions, not ordinary BMP chords.

57

The four-chord D♯dim7 pattern

The D♯dim7 chord is not so straightforward.

Here are the chord tones of the original, two-chord D sharp dim 7 chord:

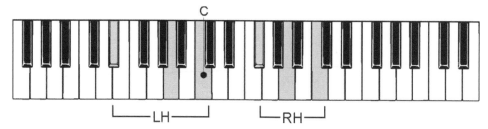

The four-chord D♯dim7 chord starts on the same note, but you can see there are many more minor third jumps:

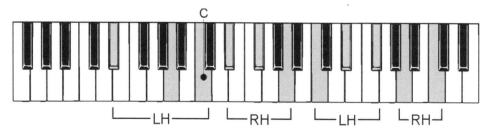

This is the music for both versions of the D♯dim7 chord:

| Pyramids_L7_A3 | Pyramids_L7_M3 |

Only the chord tones are shown, not the melody, developed or not.

Rehearsing the four-chord B section

(See next page.)

Play the zigzag B section melody and bass lines – the inside, six-eight music in the next diagram:

Then move your right hand up an octave and your left hand down to play the new, twelve-eight music. Note that the LH D# (only) is the same note.

Then all you have to do is fit in four BMP chords for each chord symbol:

The keyboard down the left-hand side of the page shows you where the lowest notes of the four chords are. The melody notes are also indicated.

Play the full Pyramids four-chord AABA version

Here is the developed B section melody from the six-eight, two chord version. (The instructions for developing the B section melody start on page 51. Review them if necessary.) Note that lower-case letters are used to indicate notes, not chords.

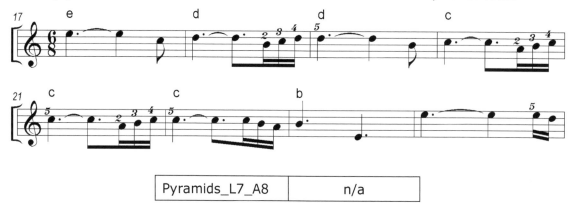

Pyramids_L7_A8	n/a

For the four-chord version, you 'stretch out' the melody, an octave higher.

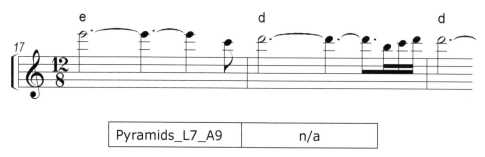

Pyramids_L7_A9	n/a

Play the four-chord B section chords with the developed melody.

Pyramids_L7_A1	Pyramids_L7_M1

The music for the developed four-chord B section is on the next page, but even if you can play from the written-out music, go through this lesson thoroughly so that you understand how the music is being created out of building blocks you already know.

Note that you now have everything you need to play an impressive four-chord AABA version of Pyramids.

Pyramids_L7_29	Pyramids_L7_29

- You have already played a 16-bar A1A2 four-chord version with developed melody.
- You have just learned the developed-melody four-chord B section (this lesson).
- You only have to play these sections in the A1A1BA2 combination for an impressive Pyramids performance.

Use any of the AABA chord charts in previous lessons to guide your performance.

Pyramids: Four-chord B Section

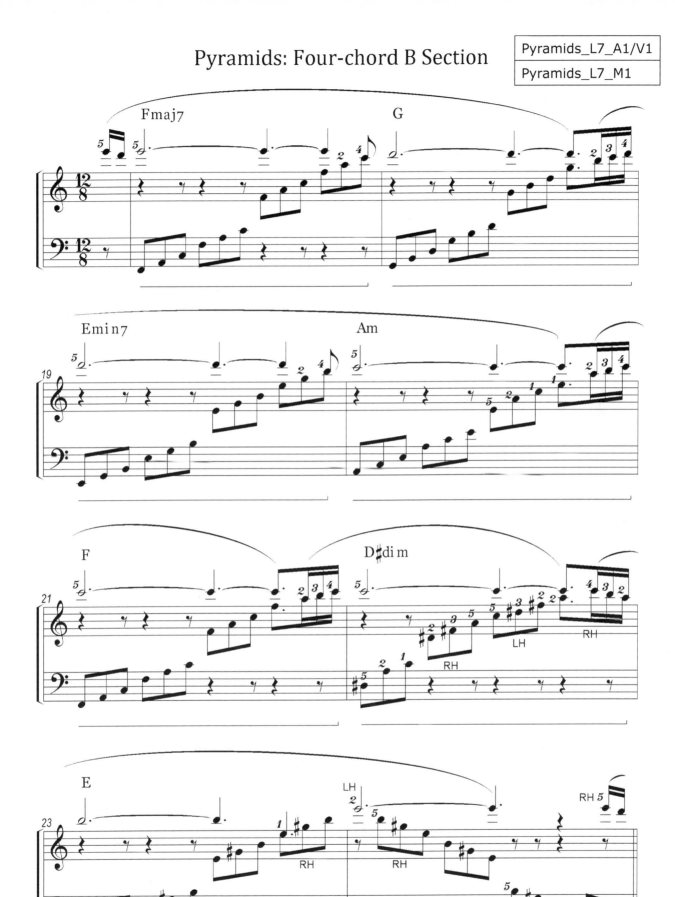

Pyramids: Concert Performance

| AUDIO 1 | MIDI 1 | Lesson performance: | Pyramids_L8_A1/V1 | Pyramids_L8_M1 |

If you have completed lessons One to Seven in this series, you can already play all the music in the Pyramids Concert Performance.

The Concert Performance consists of five 8-bar phrases in twelve-eight.

- First you play an Introduction – a four-chord A1 strain without any melody. (You learnt this in Lesson Four.)
- Then you play the 32-bar A1A1BA2 version from Lesson Seven.

Here is a chord chart of the Concert Performance:

Introduction

Am	F	G	Em	F	Dm	E	E
Four-chord patterns with no melody						LH-over pattern	

Main Sequence

A^1	Am	F	G	Em	F	Dm	E	E
	Four-chord patterns with developed melody...						LH-over pattern	

A^1	Am	F	G	Em	F	Dm	E	E
	exactly same as previous 8 bars...						LH-over pattern	

B	Fmaj7	G	Em7	Am	F	D#dim7	E	E
	B section...						LH-over pattern	

A^2	Am	F	G	Em	F	E	Am	Am
	same as A¹ up to ...					.different, + LH-over ending		

If you can remember what you learned in lessons One to Seven in this series, you should be able to play the Pyramids Concert Performance from the chord chart right away.

You will find the music for the Concert Performance on page 64 on, but it is important to try to play the music from the chord chart or purely from memory. (Note that the repeat of the A¹ strain is indicated by repeat marks: ⦂   ⦂)

If you can read music well, study the music so that you can see how the chord chart represents it, and then use the chord chart on its own.

Make your performance expressive

The music does not have performance markings like tempo and 'dynamics' (loudness and softness indications). This is because the Musicarta method is designed to help you play less from written-out music and more from your own knowledge and artistic impulse.

You must put those shadings in yourself. Of course, you will try to 'bring out the melody'. It is also usual to try to make the B section different in some way, and slow down and fade away at the end.

If you want a really musical performance, spend some time imagining what you yourself would like to hear. What orchestral instruments would you use if you could conduct an orchestra playing the Concert Performance? If the Pyramids music were a film soundtrack, what would be happening on screen? Imagine a concert pianist playing the Pyramids variations in the most outrageously 'artistic' manner possible – an aim for that performance.

Pyramids: Concert Performance

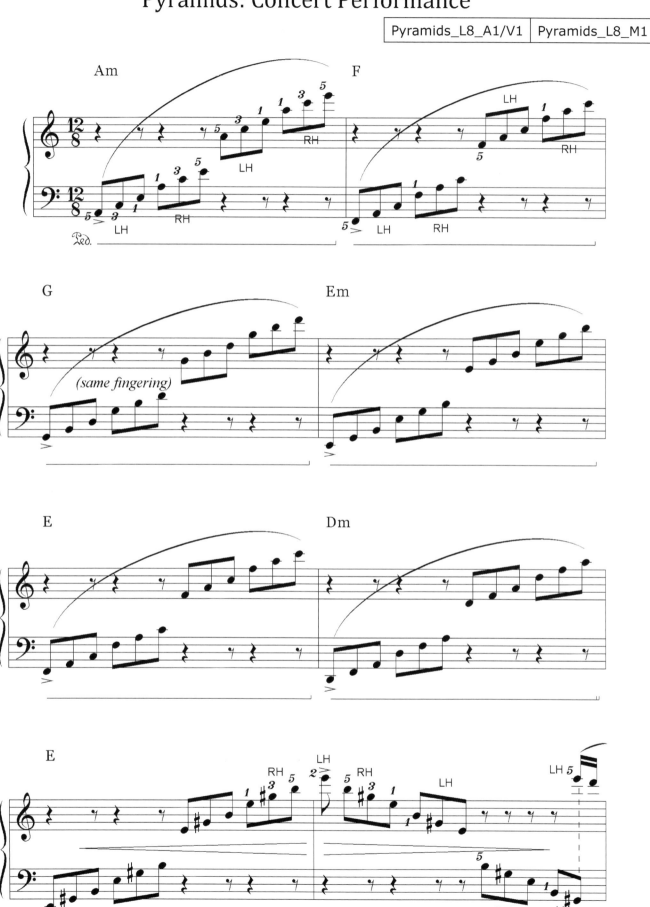

A Variation-type performance

Make the most of the work you have put into learning Pyramids by playing the full Concert Version at the end of a build-up from the simpler versions.

For example, you could play:

- Pyramids with LH-over Patterns (two-chord, 16-bar A^1A^2)   (page 19)
- Two-chord AABA performance with developed melody   (page 54)

Segue into:

- Pyramids Concert Performance   (page 64)

To finish, segue into:

- An eight-bar, two-chord A2 with simplest melody to finish. (Reprise.)

In music, segue [seg-wey] means 'transition without a break into the next section of music or piece'. You could make the last note A of one version the first note A of the next, For example, here's a sketch of the segue into the Reprise.

Part Two: Supplementary Material

Pyramids in Basic Music-making Position visual prompt sheet

The chord sequence:

1							8	
Am ↘	F ↗	G ↘	Em ↗	F ↗	Dm ↗	E*	E* ↗

9							16	
Am ↘	F ↗	G ↘	Em ↗	F ↘	E* ↗	Am	Am

A sample BMP chord – A minor (Am):

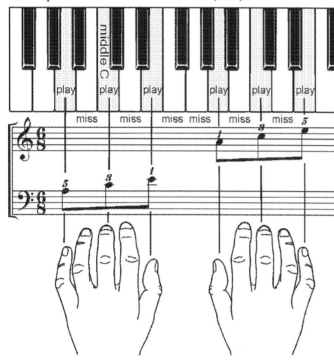

E minor (Em) and E major (E*) chords:

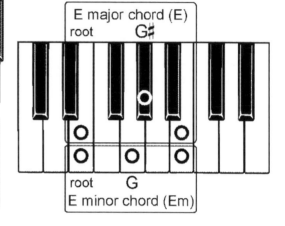

The shape the roots make:

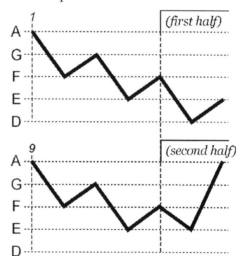

The roots of the chords shown on the keyboard:

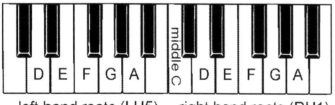

left hand roots (LH5)   right hand roots (RH1)

The first few bars with the roots indicated, showing the six-eight rhythm count:

Pyramids: Adding the Melody visual prompt sheet

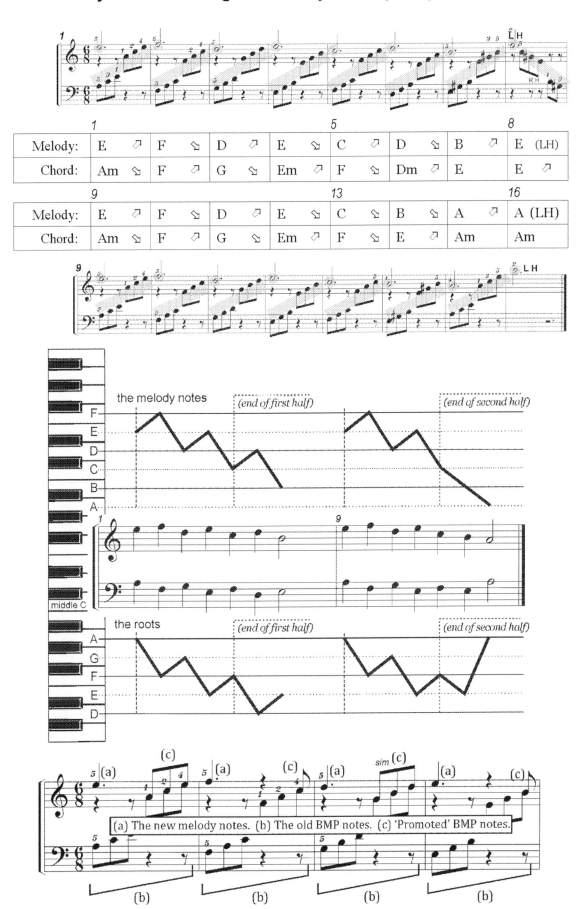

	1							5					8	
Melody:	E	↗	F	↘	D	↗	E	↘	C	↗	D	↘	B	↗	E (LH)
Chord:	Am	↘	F	↗	G	↘	Em	↗	F	↘	Dm	↗	E		E ↗

	9							13					16	
Melody:	E	↗	F	↘	D	↗	E	↘	C	↘	B	↘	A	↗	A (LH)
Chord:	Am	↘	F	↗	G	↘	Em	↗	F	↘	E	↗	Am		Am

(a) The new melody notes. (b) The old BMP notes. (c) 'Promoted' BMP notes.

Memorising the Pyramids Chord Sequence

It's easier to play Pyramids without delays if you know the chord sequence by heart. You will also enjoy playing more when you are sure of the chord sequence. Also, improvising is nearly impossible without knowing the chord sequence by heart.

Memorising the line the roots make

Because all the chords used in the build-up to the Concert Performance are simple BMP chords with the root (the name-note) at the bottom, if you learn the line the roots of the chords make, you will learn the chord sequence as well.

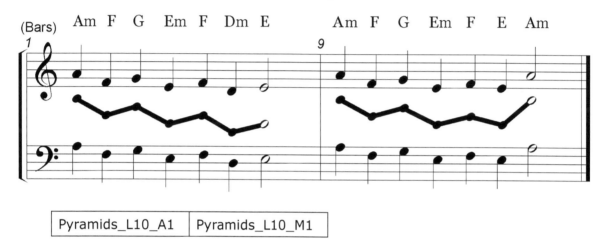

| Pyramids_L10_A1 | Pyramids_L10_M1 |

This little study, which squeezes all 16 bars of Pyramids into one line of music, lets you see and rehearse the zigzag shape the roots make as you play through the chord sequence.

Play this study using just your first fingers. Using the same finger for all the notes makes you more aware of the size and direction of the jumps.

You don't even have to read the music – the notes you play are the notes named by the chord symbol. Here they are, shown on a keyboard:

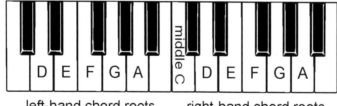

left-hand chord roots right-hand chord roots

Play the bass line over and over again saying the names of the roots as you play them.

It helps to sing the bass line. You don't have to be able to sing at all well – you just have to try to get the overall shape right.

Using the shape of the bass line to help you

Here is the zigzag line the bass notes make, squashed and stretched so that you can see its shape more clearly.

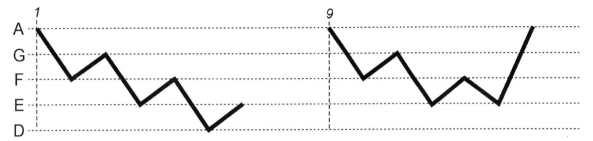

Different people remember things in different ways. You might find the following activities help you memorise the bass line, and thus the chord sequence.

- Trace the zigzag shape of the bass line with your finger. Memorise the shape.
- Draw the zigzag bass line in your mind's eye as you hum the bass line to yourself.
- Play the bass line with your index fingers again, observing how the sound has the same 'shape' as the zigzag bass line.

The bass line ladder

In the next diagram, the roots are arranged vertically, so what is higher up on the page is a higher note too. The arrowed line shows the movement of the roots in the first and second halves of a 16-bar Pyramids version.

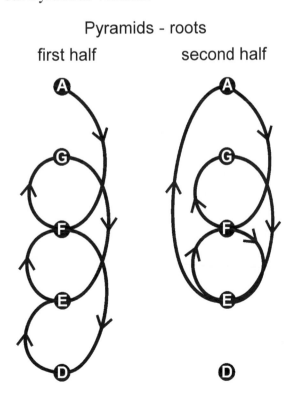

Pyramids - roots

first half   second half

73

Check that you can see how the lines follow the roots:

First half: A – F – G – E – F – D – E

Second half: A – F – G – E – F – E – A

To help you memorise the chord sequence, tap the roots on the 'blank' diagram below with your finger as you sing or hum the bass line tune to yourself. You don't actually have to follow the curly shape in the first diagram as long as you tap the dots in order.

Pyramids – roots ladder
for tapping
(use for both halves)

A

G

F

E

D

After a few goes with your eyes open, do the exercise with your eyes closed. Sing the bass line and tap the piece of paper where you think the dots are.

You won't know exactly where the dots are, but make as sure as possible that your third bass note 'G' is halfway between your 'A' and your 'F', for example, and that you jump over the imaginary 'F' to get to 'E'.

Make a special effort with the last three bass notes of each half:

A – F – G – E – [F – D – E] (end of the first half)

A – F – G – E – [F – E – A] (end of the second half)

Steps, skips and jumps

The roots of the chords move three different distances:

- a <u>step</u> – to the next-door white key, either up (right) or down (left),
- a <u>skip</u> – over the next-door key to the one beyond, or
- a <u>jump</u> – over more than one white key (bigger than a skip).

Here's a table showing the distances the Pyramids bass moves between notes.

1   *9*

skip down	step up	skip down	step up	skip down	step up	jump up	skip down	step up	skip down	step up	step down	jump up

Here is the zigzag Pyramids bass line shape marked with steps, skips and jumps:

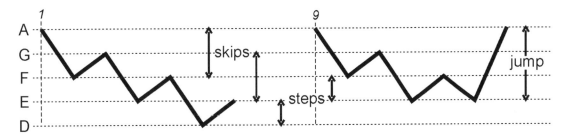

Here is the roots ladder with the size of the movements marked.

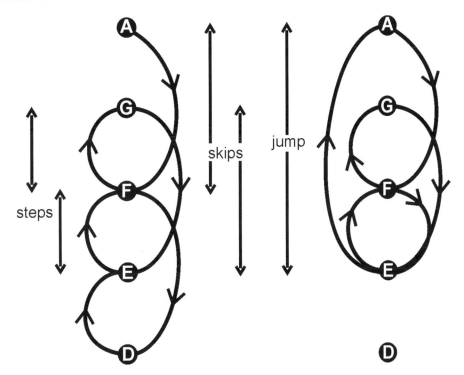

- All three diagrams on this page show the same thing. Work through them making sure you can see how the skips, steps and jumps shown in

75

the table at the top match the distances shown in the line and ladder diagrams.

- Describe the movement of the bass line to yourself in words – when it moves down and when up, and by how much.

- Do all the previous exercises calling out whether the movement is a step, a skip or a jump.

- Sing the bass line naming the sizes of the movements. Sing: "Start on A, down a skip (F), up a step (G), down a skip (E)…" and so on to the end.

Two halves with different endings

Look at the shape of the line the roots make:

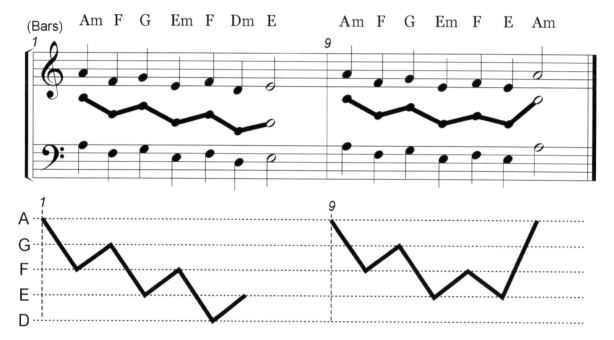

If we place the first-half shape (bars 1 to 8) above the second-half shape (bars 9 to 16), we can see that both lines are the same as far as the second F chord:

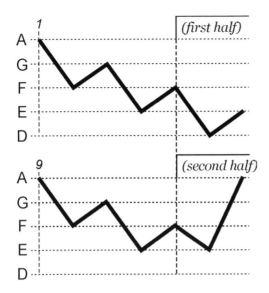

Only the endings of the lines are different.

- The last three chords of the first half are F, Dm, E
- The last three chords of the second half are F, E, Am

If you can remember the different way the two halves end, you can probably remember the whole sequence.

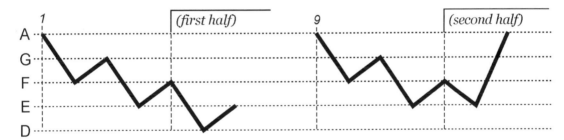

Here is your exercise:

- Play or hum the bass notes at the end of the first half (F, D, E), followed directly by the bass notes at the end of the second half (F, E, A).

Here's the chord sequence table again, with the end of the ends of the first and second halves highlighted:

1								(end of the first half)				
Am	⬊	F	⬈	G	⬊	Em	⬈	F	⬊	Dm ⬈	E	E ⬈

9								(end of the second half)			
Am	⬊	F	⬈	G	⬊	Em	⬈	F	⬊	E ⬈	Am	Am

Another very useful and effective exercise is to play the two different endings as you say or sing exactly what it is you are trying to learn.

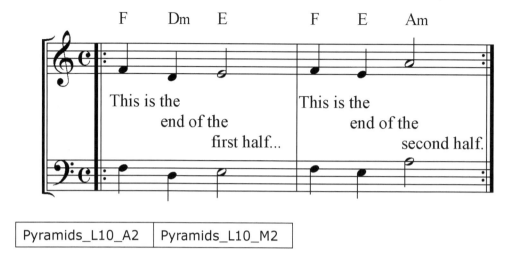

| Pyramids_L10_A2 | Pyramids_L10_M2 |

'Bringing out the bass line'

It pays to start every practice session by reminding yourself of the Pyramids chord sequence by playing the first line-of-the-roots study in this section. If your performance has any delays which show you are unsure of the chord sequence, go back and drill that part of the bass line.

Use your knowledge of the bass line in your performance. The movement of the bass line is the most interesting thing about Pyramids until the right hand tune is introduced. You should 'bring out the melody' of the bass line when you play. Give the 14 bass notes extra weight and volume and, if you can, use the pedal to connect them together in one long, singing line.

Pyramids Build-ups

The underlying structures and features of a piece of music are always simpler than the actual music, heard or seen.

By 'underlying structures and features', we mean:

(in Part One)

- the chord sequence,
- a hand position (such as the Basic Music-making Position),
- the performance 'texture', in terms of finger movement,
- the bass line and the melody line, and the shape of these, and
- the piece's musical form and possible variations and developments of it.

(in Part Three)

- chords in inversion,
- approach note movement types,
- bottom, middle, top analysis,
- together, left, right analysis, and
- standard chord sequences such as the circle of fifths.

Many ways of indicating underlying structures are presented in the Pyramids Variations volume. The more ways you use to look at these structures, the better your understanding of them and the better your chances of playing the piece with confidence and enjoyment.

Also, a reliable knowledge of underlying structures (plus the techniques for bringing them to life in performance modelled in the present volume) is essential for improvising, at any level.

Build-ups

From the point of view of learning Pyramids, revising the structures and re-building the performance every time from its simplest elements pays dividends.

A complete build-up to the Concert Performance might consist of the following elements. The actual performances are given in brackets.

79

This is a comprehensive list for demonstration purposes only, and will in practice be slimmed down and more accurately targeted. Teachers will also find it useful to address memorisation throughout, using the material and techniques in the Part Two memorisation module.

Teachers who are familiar with the Pyramids material will not find it difficult to devise similar build-ups for the variations in Part Three. Build-ups can also form the basis of 'medley' performances of the Pyramids Variations.

Part Three: Variations

Developing the Bass Line

Part One: A Pyramids Left-hand-over Version

| AUDIO 2 | MIDI 2 | Section performance: | Pyramids_DBL_A1 | Pyramids_DBL_M1 |

If you know how to find chords, you can make new musical versions of a piece working directly from the chord sequence.

For example, you have already learnt how to play left-hand-over patterns for the introduction, bars 7 and 8 and the ending of the Pyramids First Performance. You can make a new version of Pyramids using this LH-over pattern for all the chords in the chord sequence – the 'Left-hand-over Version'.

These are the piano keys you use for an A minor LH-over pattern:

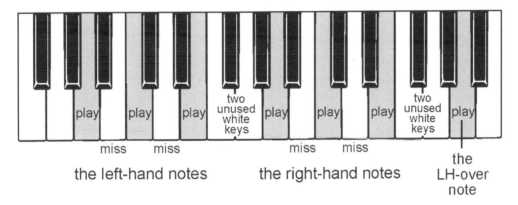

The spacing applies to all the chords in Pyramids except the E major chord, which substitutes the black G sharp for the middle chord tone in each hand.

You can see what the LH-over pattern looks like in written-out music below.

A new time signature

The LH-over pattern has twice as many notes as the six-note Basic Music-making Position pattern. If we play one LH-over pattern for each chord symbol in the Pyramids chord sequence, the LH-over Version will be twice as long as before.

Here is a LH-over pattern written out in six-eight, with the counting written in:

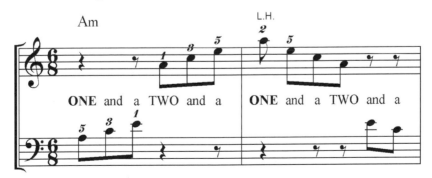

83

If we write the music for the LH-over Version 'in twelve-eight' – with twelve quavers to a bar – we can use the same chord chart as before, but play twelve notes for each chord symbol. Here is the same music written out in twelve-eight:

As you can see, we count a bar of twelve-eight:

"**ONE**–and–a TWO–and–a **THREE**–and–a FOUR–and–a…"

The notes in twelve-eight come at exactly the same speed as the notes in six-eight, so one bar of twelve-eight is twice as long as a bar of six-eight.

Playing the new LH-over Version

Try to play a LH-over Version of Pyramids, with one twelve-note LH-over pattern for each chord symbol in the chord sequence.

1					7	8
Am ↘	F ↗	G ↘	Em ↗	F ↘	Dm ↗	E	E ↗

9					15	16
Am ↘	F ↗	G ↘	Em ↗	F ↘	E ↗	Am	Am

Notice that:

- The last note of a LH-over pattern is the middle note of the left hand chord. You jump from there to the root (name-note) of the next chord.

- In bars 7 and 8 you play two LH-over patterns – one for each E major chord symbol.

- Listen carefully to your ending (bars 15 and 16), to make sure it's neither too long nor too short. One-and-a-half bars is a good length.

Remember to play E major chords in bars 7, 8 and 14. Try to play the LH-over Version without music, if you possibly can. Here is a sample to work from.

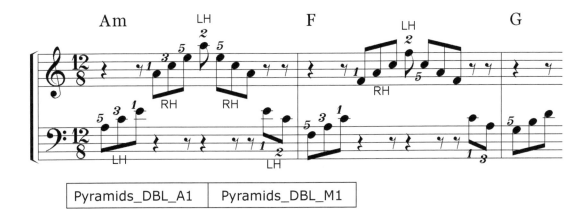

| Pyramids_DBL_A1 | Pyramids_DBL_M1 |

A 10-note left-hand-over pattern

Because the last note of a LH-over pattern is the middle note of the left-hand BMP chord, some of the joins between the patterns don't sounds quite right. The middle note of a BMP chord is not a good final note for a pattern, as we found when we were looking for a LH-over ending (page 16).

One thing we can do is make the RH thumb (on the way down) the last note of the LH-over pattern (as we did for one of our left-hand-over endings). This gives us a 10-note LH-over pattern, and two empty quaver 'slots' at the end of each bar.

We are going to use these two empty slots to turn the zigzag Pyramids bass line (the line of the lowest notes) into more of a tune. But first, play through the Pyramids chord sequence using 10-note LH-over patterns. The first two bars are written out as an example, below.

(You can still use full 12-note LH-over patterns in bars 7 and 15, where the chord stays the same over the bar line.)

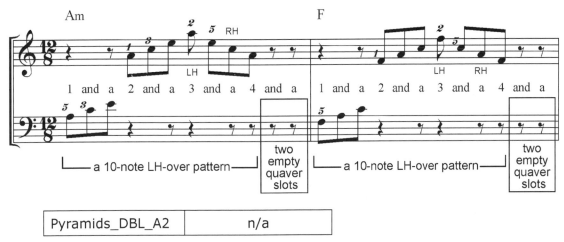

| Pyramids_DBL_A2 | n/a |

Part Two: Developing the Bass Line

AUDIO 2	MIDI 2	Section performance:	Pyramids_DBL_A6/V6	Pyramids_DBL_M6

The bass line of a piece of music is the musical line that the lowest notes of a piece of music make. (Electric bass guitars and the string double bass often play the bass lines in popular music.) The notes of the bass line are usually the roots of the chords of the chord sequence, plus some notes in between to make the bass notes into a more interesting musical line.

The Pyramids bass line – the zigzag pattern of the chord roots – is already quite noticeable. We are going to use the two empty quaver slots at the end of the ten-note LH-over pattern to make it more musical, by filling them with little bass-line tunes which approach the next root in an interesting way.

Bass line movement types.

Let's look at the possibilities in the first two chord changes.

We'll repeat the root of the current chord in the first of the two quaver slots, so that the listener remembers where we're coming from. That leaves just one quaver slot before the root of the next chord, shown here by the question mark:

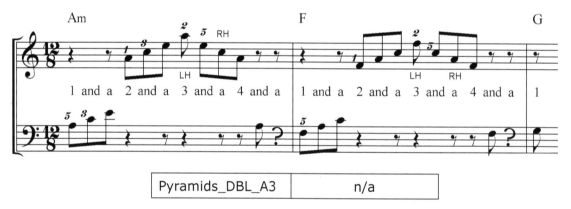

Pyramids_DBL_A3	n/a

White key G, between root A and root F, seems an obvious choice. We'll put it in and call this three-note approach movement 'Type One'.

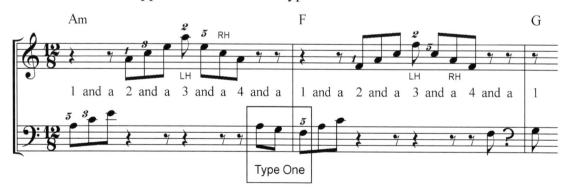

86

Pyramids_DBL_A4	n/a

Type One movement walks by steps* to the next root.

Type One – step/step

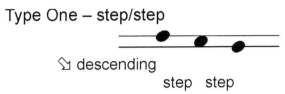

↘ descending

step   step

*A step in music is a movement to a note with a next-door letter-name: an F to a G, a C to a B, etc. Step-wise movement is always desirable in music – it's 'easy on the ear'.

Look at the next chord change (F to G). There isn't a white key between the repeated root F and our target note, the next root, G. Instead, jump over our target note to the note beyond (A) and fall back to the new root on the first beat of the new bar. We will call this approach movement 'Type Two'.

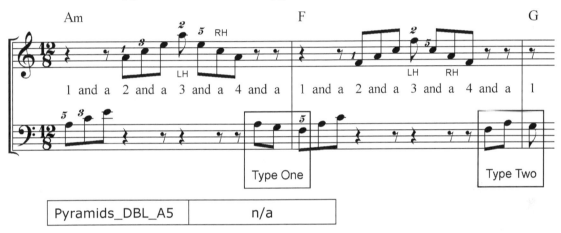

Pyramids_DBL_A5	n/a

Type Two movement skips* to the other side of the target note (the next root), and then steps back to arrive. Notice these are again all small steps.

Type Two – skip/step

↗ ascending

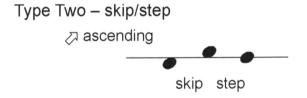

skip   step

*A skip movement 'skips over' one note letter-name to the note with the letter-name just the other side: an F to an A, or a G to a B (skipping A), for example.

A first developed bass line

Movement patterns Types One and Two on their own are enough to develop nearly the whole bass line, as you can see in the chart that follows. Use full, 12-note LH-over patterns at the end of the first half, and one-and-a-half 12-note LH-over patterns for the ending.

Developed bass line

Am		F		G		Em		F		Dm		E	E
	Type One ↘	Type Two ↗		Type One ↘		Type Two ↗		Type One ↘		Type Two ↗		two 12-note LH-over patterns	

Am		F		G		Em		F		E		Am	Am
	Type One ↘	Type Two ↗		Type One ↘		Type Two ↗		?		One-and-a-half 12-note LH-over patterns for an ending			

Pyramids_DBL_A6	Pyramids_DBL_M6

These are the approach movements in use so far

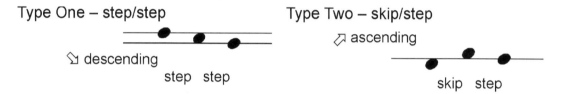

Type One – step/step
↘ descending
step   step

Type Two – skip/step
↗ ascending
skip   step

You need to work out how Type One gets you from G to E (bars 3 to 4). Remember that 'Type One movement walks by steps to the next root'. You need to work out how Type Two gets you from E to F (bars 4 to 5). Remember that 'Type Two movement skips to the other side of the target note then steps back to arrive'. Play the LH-over Version with the developed bass line as far as you can.

Finally, we need a solution for the last empty cell in the table – F to E, bars 13 to 14.

Before, when there wasn't a note between the roots (for example, F to G, bars 2 to 3), we used Type Two, ascending:

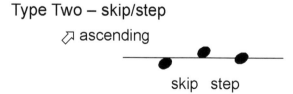

Type Two – skip/step
↗ ascending
skip   step

Here, we have the same situation, but going down (descending) instead of up, so we need to turn Type Two the other way up to get 'Type Two, descending':

Type Two – skip/step

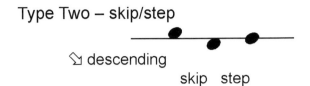

↷ descending

skip   step

Across bars 13 to 14, the bass line will move like this:

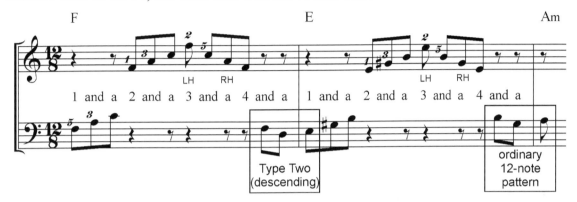

Now you can play a complete developed bass line version from this chord chart:

Developed bass line, Types One and Two

Am		F		G		Em		F		Dm		E		E	
Type One	↘	Type Two	↗	Type One	↘	Type Two	↗	Type One	↘	Type Two	↗	ordinary 12-note LH-over patterns			

Am		F		G		Em		F		E		Am		Am	
Type One	↘	Type Two	↗	Type One	↘	Type Two	↗	Type Two	↘	ordinary 12-note LH-over patterns and ending					

Pyramids_DBL_A6	Pyramids_DBL_M6

Here is a reminder of the approach movements that are being used.

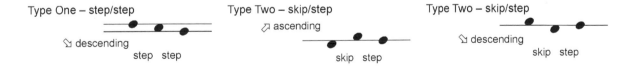

The music for the developed bass line using movement Types One and Two is on the next page.

Pyramids: Developed Bass Line, Types One and Two

A Type Three bass line movement

When there's no room for an 'in-between note', we use Type Two movement, which skips to the other side of the target note and then steps back to arrive.

We can use the same trick even if there is room for an in-between note. The bass line will jump more than one note to the other side of the target note, then step back. This is our new Type Three approach movement – jump/step.

Type Three – jump/step

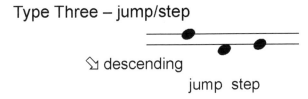

Here are the first three bars of a bass line that uses a mix of movement Types One, Two and Three. The middle part of each bar has been cut out to fit the example into one line of music. You will supply the missing part of the LH-over pattern yourself.

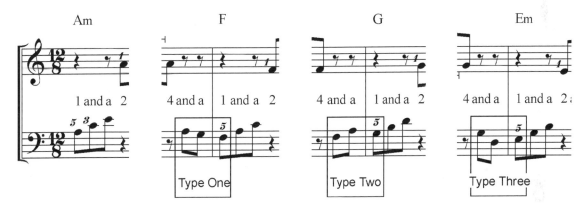

This is the chord chart for the whole of this version:

Developed bass line, mixed Types One, Two and Three

Am		F		G		Em		F		Dm		E	E
	Type One	⇘	Type Two	⇗	Type Three	⇘	Type Two	⇗	Type One	⇘	Type Two	⇗	ordinary 12-note LH-over patterns

Am		F		G		Em		F		E		Am	Am
	Type One	⇘	Type Two	⇗	Type Three	⇘	Type Two	⇗	Type Two	⇘	ordinary 12-note LH-over pattern and ending	

Pyramids_DBL_A7	Pyramids_DBL_M7

We can make another bass line using only movement Types Two and Three:

Developed bass line, Types Two and Three only

Am		F		G		Em		F		Dm		E		E
Type Three	⬐	Type Two	⬀	Type Three	⬐	Type Two	⬀	Type Three	⬐	Type Two	⬀	ordinary 12-note LH-over patterns		

Am		F		G		Em		F		E		Am		Am
Type Three	⬐	Type Two	⬀	Type Three	⬐	Type Two	⬀	Type Two	⬐	ordinary 12-note LH-over pattern and ending			

Pyramids_DBL_A8	Pyramids_DBL_M8

Here are the approach movements you need (apart from the ordinary 12-note LH-over patterns) for these versions:

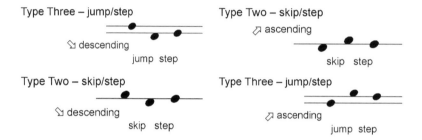

Check the movement types against the two developed bass line tables on the previous page. The first note in each bar is always the same note as the letter in the chord symbol, so you can play them without really reading the music.

Part Three: Bass lines in six-eight with RH first inversion chords

AUDIO 2	MIDI 2	Performance:	Pyramids_DBL_A11 on	Pyramids_DBL_M11

It's a good idea to sketch these developed bass lines in six-eight. You can hear the musical logic of the line a lot better and develop your ideas more easily without the long wait in the twelve-eight bar.

You can still 'stretch out' these bass lines and play them in twelve-eight. But if you learn right hand 'first inversion chords' for the Pyramids chord sequence, you can play these developed bass lines in six-eight. This will make experimenting a lot quicker and more efficient, as well as giving you another Pyramids variation to play.

First inversion Pyramids chords

The official name for a Basic Music-making Position (BMP) chord is 'a triad in root position' – 'triad' because it has three notes (like tripod and tricycle), and 'root position', which tells us the lowest note is the root (the name-note).

We can tip root position triads upside down and get other useful chords called inversions. If we take the bottom note and move it up an octave – to the next note of the same letter name, we get a first inversion chord, with the root at the top. The other two notes stay in the same place.

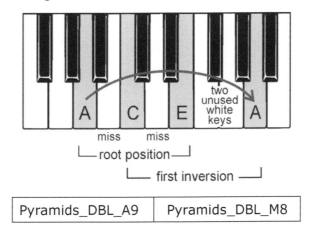

Note that the new top note is also the 'LH-over note' in the LH-over pattern:

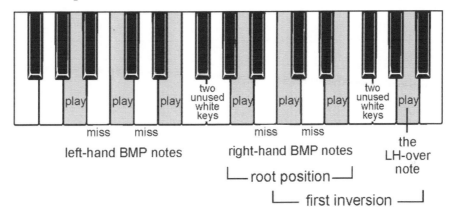

To make this new version of Pyramids using first inversion chords, we need first inversions of all the right hand BMP chords in the Pyramids chord sequence.

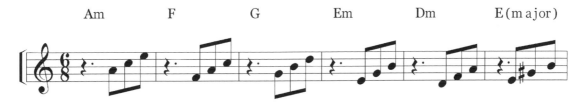

To find the inversions, first we 'squash' the broken chords back into line:

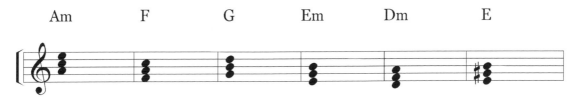

Then we move the lowest note (the root, or name-note) up an octave, to the top. The

93

other two notes stay in the same place. The root position chord becomes the first inversion of the same chord.

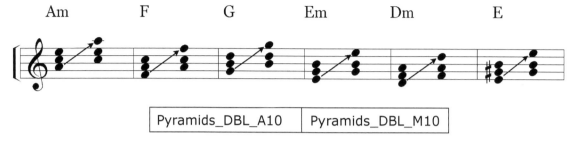

| Pyramids_DBL_A10 | Pyramids_DBL_M10 |

Looking more closely at a few examples:

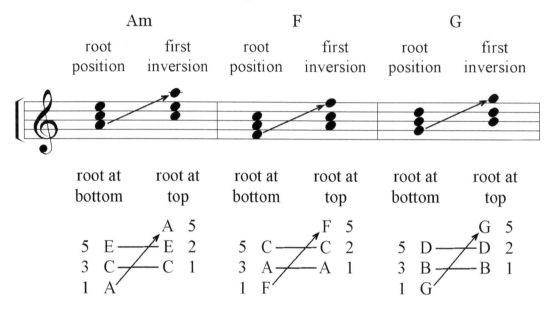

Notice that you are asked to use right hand finger 2 for the middle note of the first inversion chord, instead of finger 3. This helps keep the back of the hand flat. Make an effort to get into the habit of using finger 2 for right-hand first inversion chords.

Next, spread the first inversion chords back out, leaving quaver slots for the root and the two 'movement type' approach notes in the left hand. Here is an example.

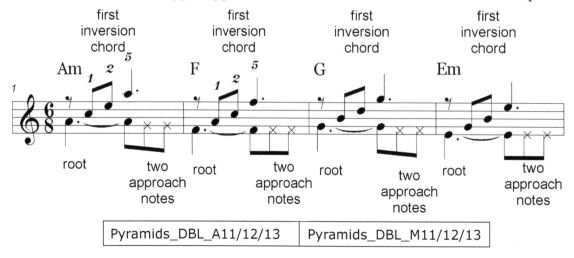

| Pyramids_DBL_A11/12/13 | Pyramids_DBL_M11/12/13 |

Notice these three things:

- The music is all written on one treble clef stave. You have not seen the bass line written in the treble clef before, but the first note in the bar is always the chord root, named in the chord symbol.

- The stems-up notes in the music are the right hand notes – the first inversion chords. The stems-down notes are the left hand developed bass line notes.

- The left hand plays only the bass line notes, and no chords. The right hand plays only the new first inversion chords.

The phantom cross-head notes stand for any of the movement type approach notes you choose.

Developed bass lines to play with RH first inversion chords

There are already three complete developed bass lines which you can now play in six-eight in the treble clef with right hand first inversion chords.

Developed bass line, Types One and Two

Am	F	G	Em	F	Dm	E	E
Type One ↘	Type Two ↗	Type One ↘	Type Two ↗	Type One ↘	Type Two ↗	LH-over pattern	

Am	F	G	Em	F	E	Am	Am
Type One ↘	Type Two ↗	Type One ↘	Type Two ↗	Type Two ↘	LH-over ending		

Pyramids_DBL_A11	Pyramids_DBL_M11

Developed bass line, mixed Types One, Two and Three

(The music this chart represents is shown written out on page 97.)

Am		F		G		Em		F		Dm		E	E
Type One	⬂	Type Two	⬈	Type Three	⬂	Type Two	⬈	Type One	⬂	Type Two	⬈	LH-over pattern	

Am		F		G		Em		F		E		Am	Am
Type One	⬂	Type Two	⬈	Type Three	⬂	Type Two	⬈	Type Two	⬂	LH-over ending			

Pyramids_DBL_A12	Pyramids_DBL_M12

Developed bass line, Types Two and Three only

Am		F		G		Em		F		Dm		E	E
Type Three	⬂	Type Two	⬈	Type Three	⬂	Type Two	⬈	Type Three	⬂	Type Two	⬈	LH-over pattern	

Am		F		G		Em		F		E		Am	Am
Type Three	⬂	Type Two	⬈	Type Three	⬂	Type Two	⬈	Type Two	⬂	LH-over ending			

Pyramids_DBL_A13	Pyramids_DBL_M13

Here is a reminder of the approach movements used:

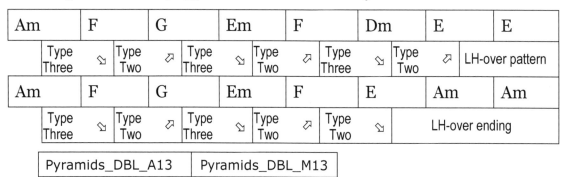

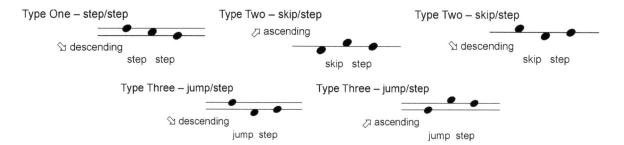

96

Pyramids: Developed Bass Line with RH First Inversion Chords
(Mixed Types One, Two and Three)

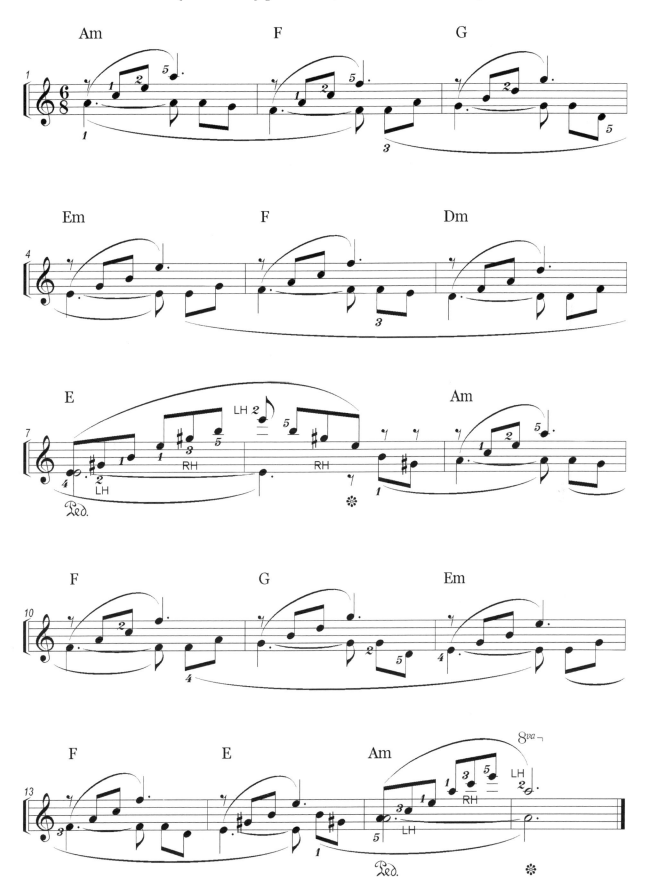

Some other bass line patterns

You can create many different bass lines by making simple rules about how the approach notes are allowed to move.

We'll explore these possible variations in six-eight in the treble clef. For a longer version, you can always stretch the bass line out to fill the gaps between 10-note LH-over patterns in twelve-eight, with the left hand in the bass clef and the hands an octave lower in their original position.

Here are some of the new rules we might try out. First, let's first scrap the rule that says we have to repeat the existing root note in the first quaver slot. Now we have two quaver slots to experiment with.

New Rule One

- Use only Basic Music-making Position (BMP) chord tones, but never use the same note twice in a row.

Here is the bass line this rule produces:

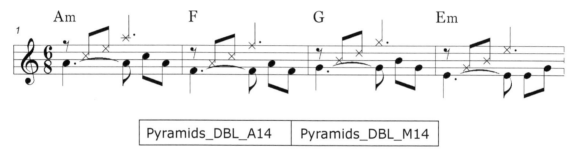

| Pyramids_DBL_A14 | Pyramids_DBL_M14 |

Try to finish the whole chord sequence like this.

If we drop the part of New Rule One which says "never use the same note twice in a row", we could create the following variation, where the bass note repeats in the even-numbered bars (2, 4, and so on).

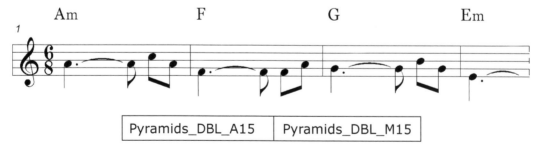

| Pyramids_DBL_A15 | Pyramids_DBL_M15 |

Place the right hand first inversion chords as before and finish the bass line. Does the movement in the even-numbered bars sounds better than before? These little differences make the bass lines more interesting for the listener. Notice that the bass line suggested here has a two-bar repeating pattern, where the odd-numbered bars follow one pattern, and the even-numbered bars follow another.

New Rule Two

New Rule Two is:

- Approach the new root using only steps.

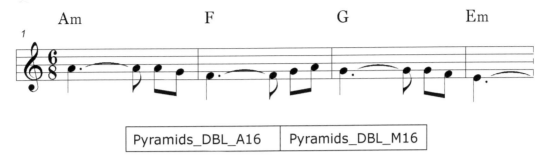

New Rule Two also generates the following variation. (The different movement is in the even-numbered bars.)

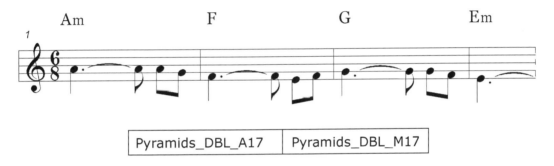

Add the right hand first inversion chords and carry these two patterns right through the chord sequence.

More bass lines, combining different movements

The best bass lines combine different types of approach movement. Here are the first bars of some examples. Both are two-bar patterns, with one type of approach movement in the odd-numbered bars, and another type in the even-numbered bars. Work out what the two movement patterns are and complete the bass lines.

New Rule Three

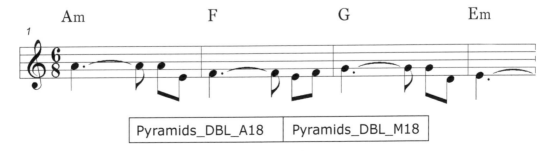

New Rule Four

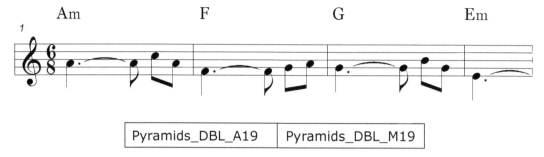

| Pyramids_DBL_A19 | Pyramids_DBL_M19 |

In the end, you will probably decide on a favourite bass line which combines several different movements. "Because I like it!" is a perfectly good 'rule', although sometimes the deciding factor will be that you feel a particular type of movement in a certain place definitely doesn't work. (Rule: "Because I don't like it!")

As an exercise, stretch out all these bass lines out to fill the gaps between 10-note LH-over patterns in twelve-eight, as at the start of this module.

Chord sequence and roots

Here is a reminder of the chord sequence and the pattern of the roots:

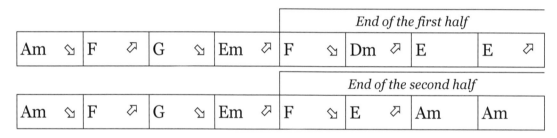

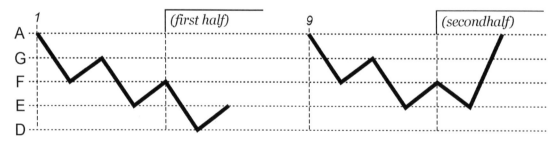

(Remember that comparing the different endings of the first and second halves of Pyramids helps you remember the Pyramids chord sequence.)

On the next page, you will find some visual cues to help you with 'flipping' your root position chords into first inversion. On the page after that you will find two developed bass lines in six-eight time written an octave lower than the other examples in this section. Play the right hand first inversion chord an octave lower as well and see if you prefer the sound.

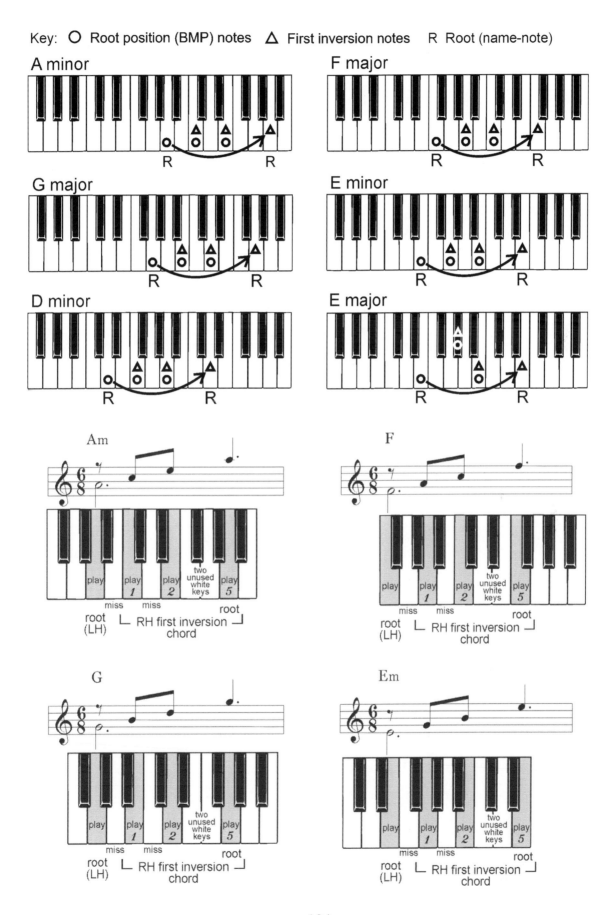

Developed bass line, mixed Types One, Two and Three

Developed bass line, Types Two and Three only

Improvising bass lines

There are two benefits from studying the ways that the bass can move between roots in such detail. The first is that thinking about and listening for steps, skips and jumps in music will help you work out by ear any music you want to play, whether it's in your head or on a CD. Does the melody or the bass line stay on the same note, or go up or down? By how much? A little or a lot? A step, a skip or a jump?

The second benefit is that playing lots of slightly different variations of the same thing prepares you to improvise. Improvising is the ability to play music that you hear in your head, but remember that we are not picking the notes out of thin air. We are improvising on a chord sequence, with known 'target notes' (the roots), moving in well-rehearsed ways.

A good 'half-way house' in improvising is to confidently play options from a well-rehearsed set even if you don't know exactly what the result will sound like. The bass line approach note movement types are just such a set of options.

Finally, remember that you cannot learn to improvise unless you are willing to make a few mistakes along the way!

Note to teachers: Bars 7 and 8, 15 and 16 using first inversions

For the ends of the two halves of Pyramids, the chord charts recommend using the original LH-over pattern – the two root position chords with a LH-over note.
At the end of the first half:

And at the end of the second half:

In practice, you will tend to repeat the RH first inversion chord in bar 8 and pass the LH over in search of further e major chord tones (see next MS example). This is, of course, quite 'correct'. The important thing is appreciating that some E major chord tones are required to fill out the bars and complete the LH-over pattern.

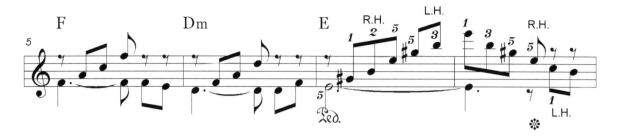

Using a first inversion in the LH is quite logical at the end of the second half:

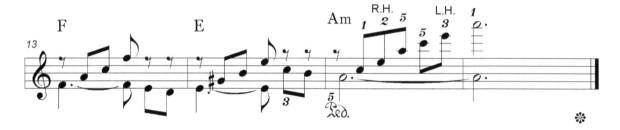

Adding the developed bass line to the Pyramids First Performance

The next challenge is to play developed bass lines under the BMP First Performance. The Pyramids First Performance can be played in the treble clef, as shown below, or the whole piece can be taken down an octave.

The left hand plays the BMP chord tones and then, as the right hand plays its BMP chord tones, it plays the moving bass line approach notes.

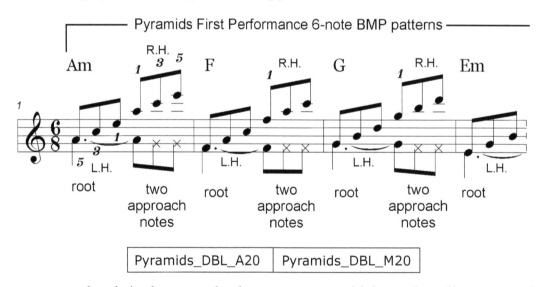

| Pyramids_DBL_A20 | Pyramids_DBL_M20 |

The cross note-heads in the example above represent whichever bass line approach notes are selected. Try playing all the six-eight bass lines we have developed under the original Pyramids First Performance six-note BMP pattern.

Advanced pupils can try to add the melody, either simple or developed, to the performance. You will find that performance written out in the Further Variations module at the end of the book.

Pyramids using Mixed Inversions

AUDIO 3 | MIDI 2 | Lesson performance: Pyramids_MX_A5/V5 | Pyramids_MX_M5

If we raise the top note of an A minor root position triad one step, we get a first inversion chord of the next chord in the Pyramids chord sequence – F major. The same is true of the G major and F major root position triads.

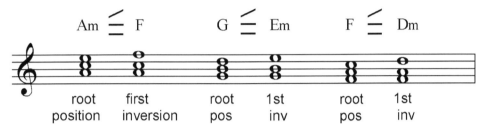

Am — F   G — Em   F — Dm

root position   first inversion   root pos   1st inv   root pos   1st inv

The little three-line diagrams between the chord symbols remind you that the two lower notes stay the same and the top one moves up. In bars 7 and 8, the bottom note of the root position E chord passes to the top to make a first inversion E chord:

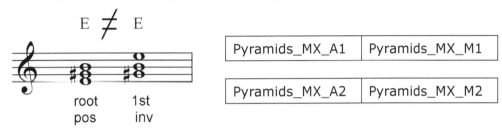

E ≠ E

root pos   1st inv

Pyramids_MX_A1	Pyramids_MX_M1

Pyramids_MX_A2	Pyramids_MX_M2

The three-line voice movement diagram shows the bottom note crossing to the top.

Putting all eight bars together, we get the same Pyramids zigzag melody line as before, but now we are seeing every note as the top note of a three-note chord.

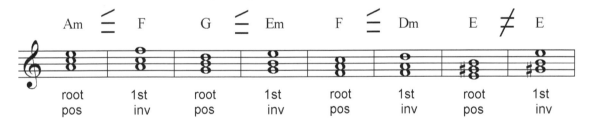

Am — F   G — Em   F — Dm   E ≠ E

root pos   1st inv   root pos   1st inv   root pos   1st inv   root pos   1st inv

Of course, if you break up the chords, you get more music out of them.

This example sounds good at a slow walking pace. The next section helps you understand what is being done, and shows how to finish this 16-bar version off.

BMT (bottom, middle, top) analysis

You will find it easier to make music out of chords if you think of their three notes as the bottom (B), middle (T) and top (T) notes. Using this 'BMT analysis', you 'see' the right hand notes like this:

Note that there are only two types of bars here: T M B T M B and T M B B M T. Sometimes the middle notes are tied and sometimes not.

We can use this BMT 'shorthand' description to indicate what happens in bars 13 to 16 (the ending) without having to write out all the notes. Try to play this:

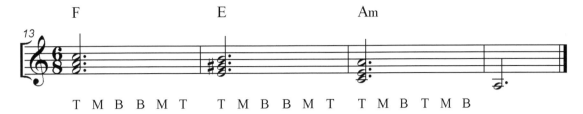

Writing music down is very time-consuming. Any shorthand you can use to avoid writing music out in full is a great idea. Also, thinking about the patterns in music rather than the individual notes generates more ideas, a lot faster.

Slash chords

In bar 8 of the music example written out on page 106, you see the chord symbol E/G♯ ("E over G sharp"). This is called a 'slash chord'. You see in the music that the chord is E major, but the bass note (in the left hand) is not the root, E. You use the 'slash chord' chord symbol to indicate that the bass note of a chord is a note other than the root. The chord symbol E/G♯ says "Play an E chord in the right hand with G sharp in the left hand." The different bass note is usually the third or the fifth.

Mixed inversions in both hands

Of course, the left hand can use root position and first inversion chords in the same

way as the right hand.

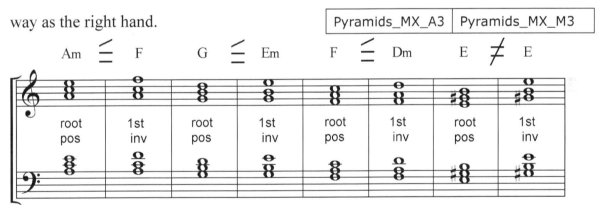

Break these two-handed chords up. Climb up the root position chords and then run down the first inversions:

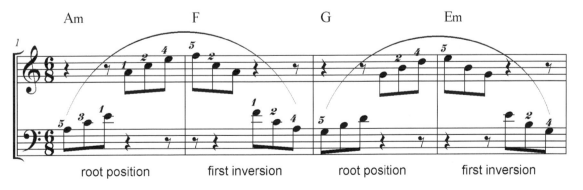

We could look at the BMT analysis of this version in a grid, to help us complete it without any written music:

	1	2	3	4
Chord	Am root pos	F first inv	G root pos	Em first inv
RH	B M T	T M B	B M T	T M B
LH	B M T	T M B	B M T	T M B

- The top line (Chord) will tell us which chord and inversion we are using.
- The middle line (RH) tells us the order to play the right hand chord tones in.
- The bottom line (LH) tells us the order to play the left hand chord tones in.

You read the whole table just like one line of music, so that it tells you which hand plays first. Check the grid against the music just above it and try to finish a 16-bar, A^1A^2 version of Pyramids using this pattern.

Then, add the tune on top of the rising/falling chord pattern:

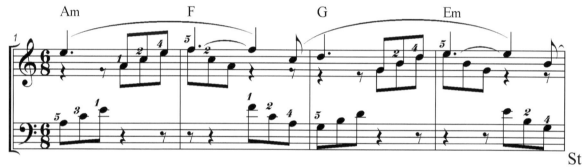

St udy the music carefully. The familiar simple Pyramids melody is at the top with the stems up, and the rising and falling pattern of the broken chords is underneath. Try to complete the version. The written-out music for both these versions follows.

Variation: Root position ascending, first inversion descending

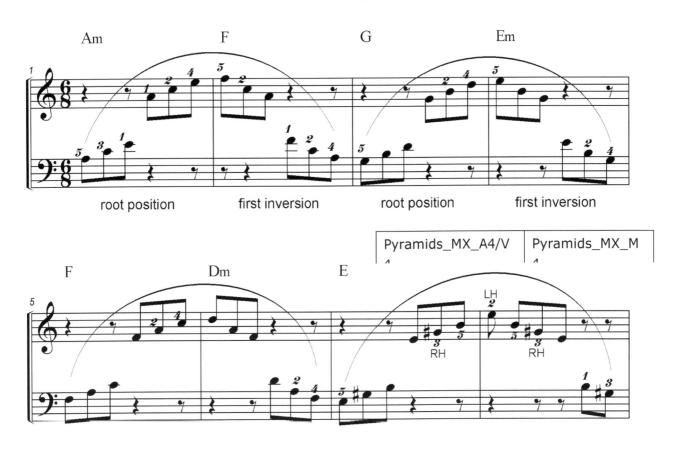

root position   first inversion   root position   first inversion

Pyramids_MX_A4/V | Pyramids_MX_M

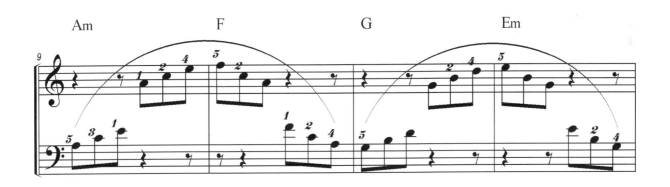

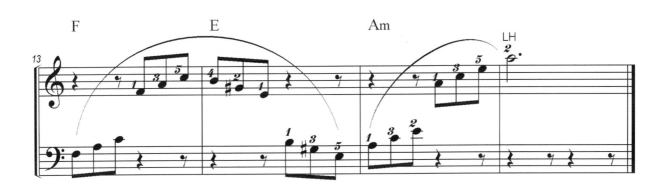

Adding the melody

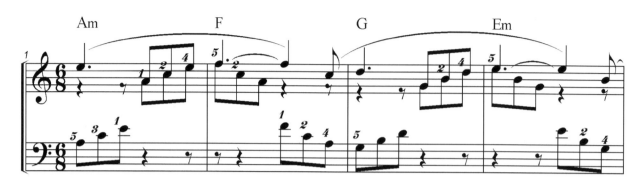

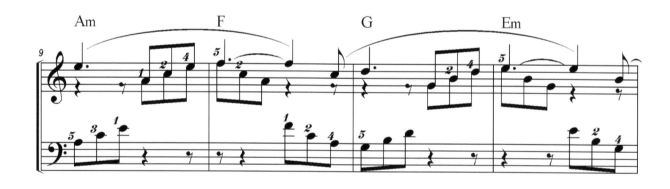

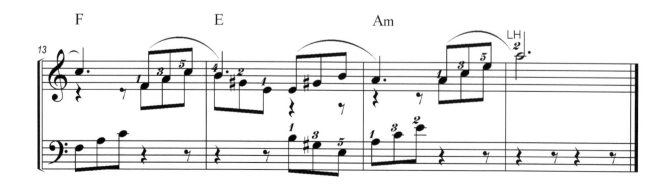

Descending Variations

AUDIO 3 | MIDI 2 | Lesson performance: | Pyramids_DV_A9/V9 | Pyramids_DV_M9

Try to play the Pyramids variation suggested in this grid:

Chord	1 Am root pos	2 F first inv	3 G root pos	4 Em first inv
RH	T M B	T M B	T M B	T M B
LH	T M B	T M B	T M B	T M B

Both hands play the same pattern (T M B) all the way through the chord sequence. The right hand plays before the left hand. Play the six notes from the highest to the lowest:

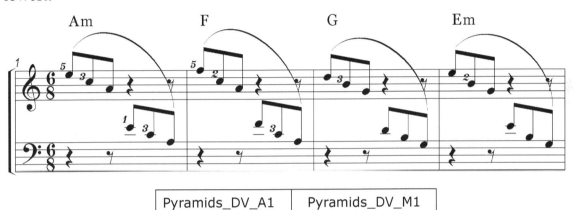

Pyramids_DV_A1 | Pyramids_DV_M1

The 'developed melody' can easily be added at the top of this pattern:

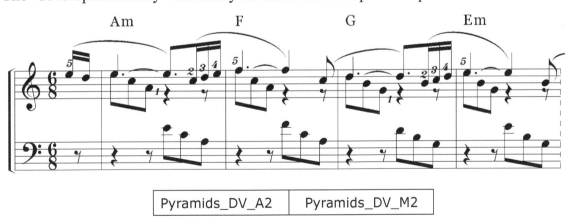

Pyramids_DV_A2 | Pyramids_DV_M2

Finish this A^1A^2 Pyramids version.

Developing the melody

This descending chord pattern provides an ideal opportunity to develop the simple Pyramids melody in the same we as we developed the bass line, using the same or very similar approach movement patterns as before:

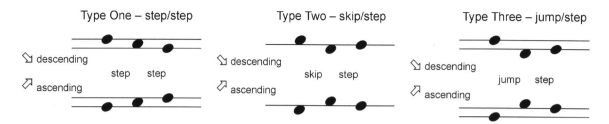

Analyse the following melody line for movement types, and play it over the Descending Variations descending chord pattern. It's a two-bar pattern.

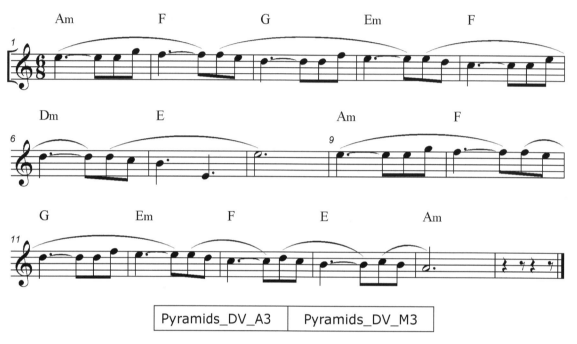

| Pyramids_DV_A3 | Pyramids_DV_M3 |

Now look at the following three patterns:

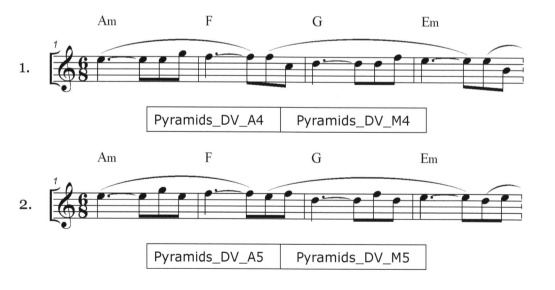

| Pyramids_DV_A4 | Pyramids_DV_M4 |

| Pyramids_DV_A5 | Pyramids_DV_M5 |

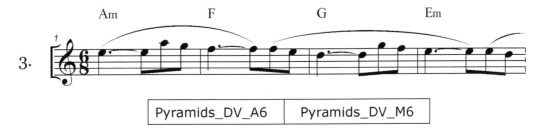

All of these are two-bar patterns – the odd-numbered bars are the same, and the even-numbered bars are the same. Decide what the pattern is, and finish the three 16-bar A^1A^2 variations.

Here are two variations with more 'approach notes', using the rhythmic pattern of the developed melody:

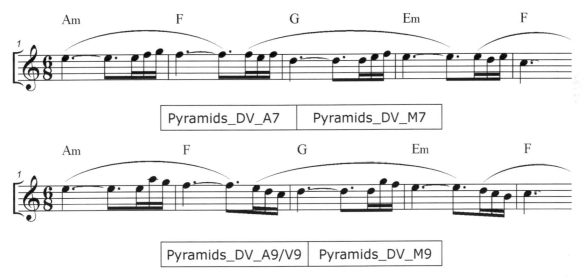

Study the examples until you can see the pattern, and finish the variations. A 32-bar AABA 'Descending Variation' follows.

Pyramids: AABA Descending Variations

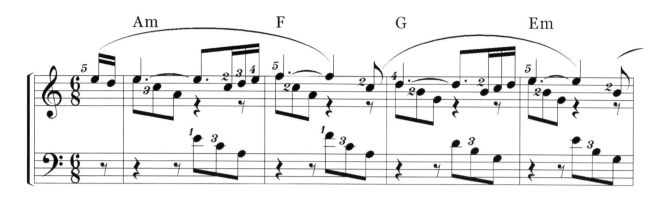

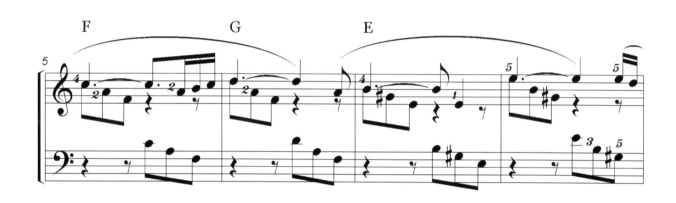

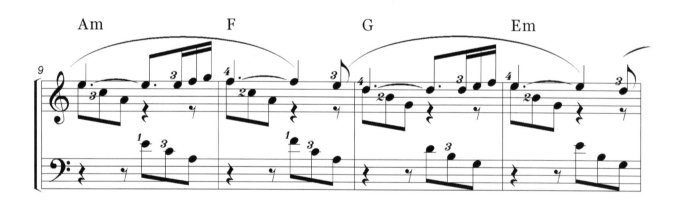

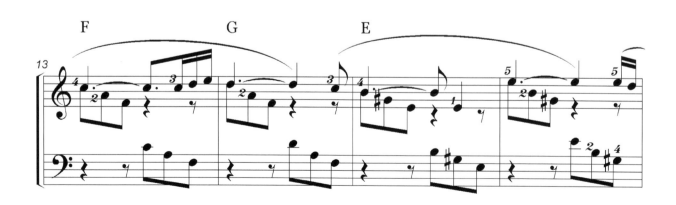

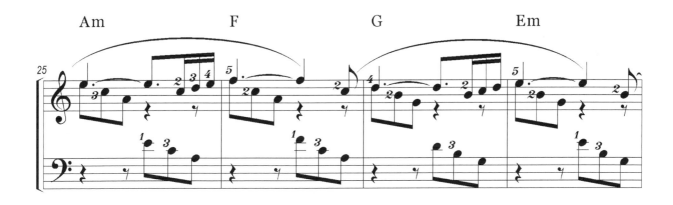

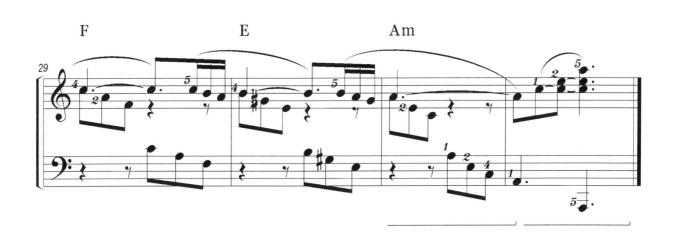

Pyramids in Four-four Time

| AUDIO 3 | MIDI 2 | Lesson performance: | Pyramids_FF_A10/V10 | Pyramids_FF_M10 |

Six-eight is not a very 'rock music' rhythm, but four-four time is. Rock music is also generally lower in pitch – further to the left on the keyboard, towards the bass, so in the first four-four version in this module, the right hand plays the chords that the left hand played in the last two modules, so the music for both hands is written in the bass clef. The left hand plays just the root of the chord.

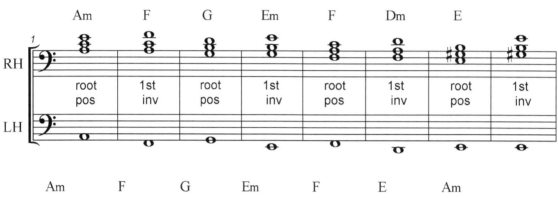

Pyramids_FF_A!   Pyramids_FF_M1

Add an even four-crotchet rhythm, at a medium walking pace:

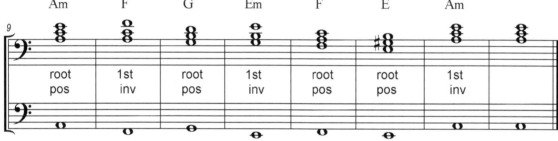

Pyramids_FF_A2   Pyramids_FF_M2

You could develop the bass line using the approach notes from the Developing the Bass Line module:

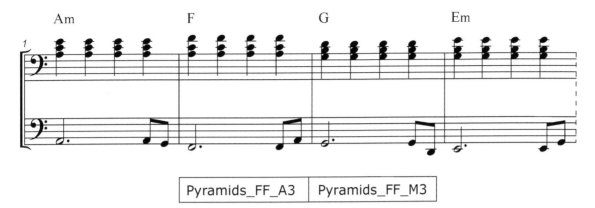

| Pyramids_FF_A3 | Pyramids_FF_M3 |

Repeat the root in the bass, on the second beat of each bar:

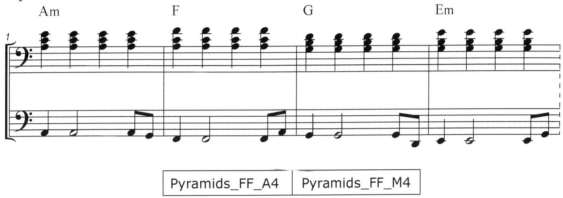

| Pyramids_FF_A4 | Pyramids_FF_M4 |

Next, try to move the added note to a syncopated (off-the-beat) position between beats two and three. The following section has some tips for learning to do this.

| Pyramids_FF_A5 | Pyramids_FF_M5 |

Syncopation and TLR (together, left, right) analysis

Playing notes off the beat (syncopated) is an important part of modern popular music style, but it can be difficult at first. Whether you are playing from the music or copying a performance, it helps to be very clear about what you are trying to play.

There are two ways to be sure, which are combined in practice. The first is counting, and the second is the TLR (together, left, right) analysis.

117

Counting

The four crotchet beats in four-four are counted one-two-three-four:

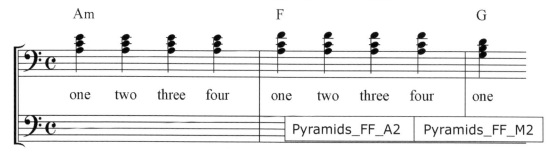

Any quavers in between are counted 'and', without changing the steady pace of the crotchet beats.

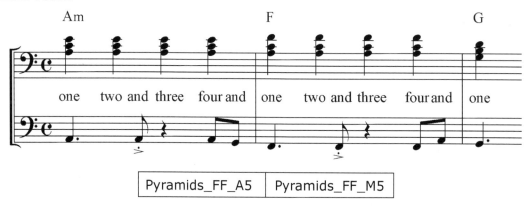

TLR analysis

TLR analysis makes it very clear whether the hands play together (T) or on their own (L/left or R/right) on the counts you have identified.

The TLR analysis of the current example shows:

It is best to teach the hands this movement without having to think about the notes or even the rhythm at first. Think of the movement of the hands as a series of 'events', and tap the series out on your desktop or the case of your keyboard. Say out loud what you expect to happen.

R	✳	✳		✳	✳		✳	✳		✳	✳			✳
	together	right	left	right	together	left	together	right	left	right	together	left	together
L	✳		✳		✳	✳	✳		✳		✳	✳	✳

The trick is to abandon the rhythm while you learn to pattern and take as long as you need between taps to be sure that what you are going to do is what the series says you must do next.

Apart from the very first 'together' beat, the events come in groups of three:

R	*		*		*		*		*		*		*		*		*
	right	left	right	,	together	left	together	,	right	left	right	,	together	left	together
L		*			*	*	*				*			*	*	*

If you say and tap these groups, you have nearly got the rhythm right.

When you come back to the keyboard to play the notes, simplify the music and repeat just the first two chords until you get the pattern right.

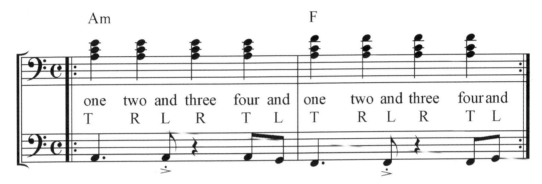

When you can play this rhythmic pattern, finish the version. You can use any of the developed bass lines from the earlier module. The approach notes come on the last two quaver beats – "four and" in the four-four rhythm.

Rock 'three plus three plus two' rhythm (3+3+2)

A bar of four-four has four crotchet beats, or eight quaver beats. In popular music, the eight quaver beats are often divided into groups of three, three and two (3+3+2).

The 3+3+2 grouping is applied to the breaking up of the chord into quavers. You can see it more clearly if you read the BMT (bottom, middle, top) analysis in the following example. (For this section, the right hand is back in the treble clef.)

Pyramids_FF_A6	Pyramids_FF_M6

119

For demonstration purposes, the quavers in the example above are beamed to the 3+3+2 rhythm, but it is more usual for them to be beamed according to the time signature, and you will have to look more carefully to see the 3+3+2 pattern:

The example above shows that the stressed (emphasised) quaver beats in a 3+3+2 bar are quavers 1, 4 and 7. You can check that you are getting the 3+3+2 rhythm right by chanting to yourself:

One two three **four** five six **seven** eight **one** two three **four** five six **seven** eight

…with extra emphasis on the bold counts.

In the next four-bar example, the bass takes up the 1, 4, 7 rhythm:

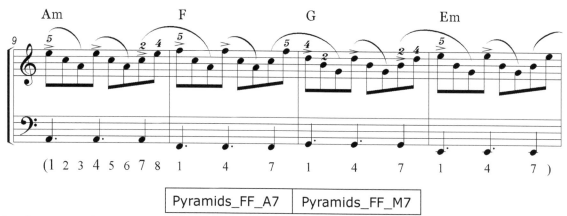

In the example which follows (the last four bars, numbers 13 to 16), the bass line is written 'properly' – according to the time signature:

Try playing a 16-bar A^1A^2 version of Pyramids with this pattern all the way through. If you can, play developed bass line approach note patterns in the bass.

Combining melody approach notes and 3+3+2 grouping

We can use the last 2-quaver group of the 3+3+2 pattern to develop the melody using the moving approach note patterns from Developing the Bass Line and Descending Variations.

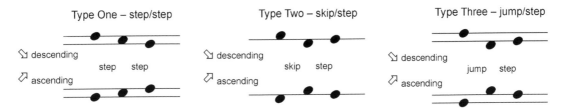

Look at the approach notes in this example carefully:

Version 1

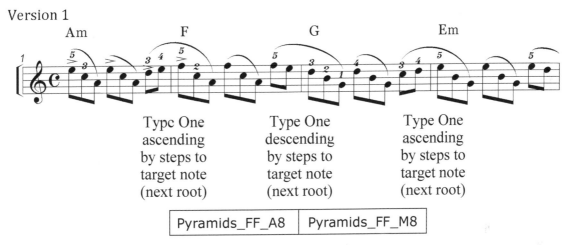

| Type One ascending by steps to target note (next root) | Type One descending by steps to target note (next root) | Type One ascending by steps to target note (next root) |

| Pyramids_FF_A8 | Pyramids_FF_M8 |

Make sure that you understand the descriptions of the approach note patterns, and complete a 16-bar A^1A^2 version, using any bass line you choose.

Do the same for the following example:

Version 2

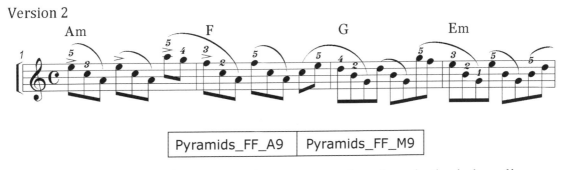

| Pyramids_FF_A9 | Pyramids_FF_M9 |

The two written-out versions are on the next page. Supply a rhythmic bass line.

Treble 3+3+2 Patterns with Approach Notes

Pyramids and the Circle of Fifths

AUDIO 4 | MIDI 2 | Lesson performance: | Pyramids_CF_A1/V1 | Pyramids_CF_M1

The circle of fifths is the most powerful chord sequence in Western music. You cannot study popular music harmony for long without learning about it. You will recognise it when you hear it, and once you know about it, you will hear it in music all the time.

The Pyramids bass line can easily be adapted to show the circle of fifths in action by lowering every other note an additional third. Look at the bass line of Pyramids as we have played it so far:

Pyramids_CF_A2 | Pyramids_CF_M2

This is the zigzag line of bass notes you have seen in many diagrams. The bass note falls a third then rises a second. Nine of the thirteen chord changes in Pyramids (underlined in the example above) follow this pattern.

Now compare the new circle of fifths bass line:

Pyramids_CF_A2 | Pyramids_CF_M2

Instead of falling a third then rising a second, the bass note now falls a fifth or rises a fourth. (Falling a fifth and rising a fourth both get you to a note of the same name.) All but the down-a-second F-to-E step is now a falling-fifth (= rising fourth) interval.

Adapting the Pyramids chord sequence

To adapt the Pyramids left hand part to show the circle of fifths, we only need to change five bass notes in a 16-bar $A^1 A^2$ version. The next music example shows the 'old' left hand version with the stems up, plus the 'new' circle of fifths version with the stems down, both on the same stave. You will play stems-down notes to create the new circle of fifths version. Notice the five bars that are different.

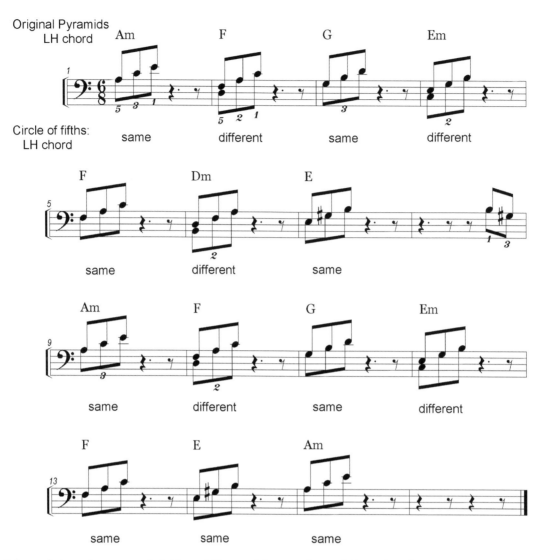

At this point, using any right hand Pyramids music and just the down-stem music above for the left hand and you could play a 16-bar circle of fifths Pyramids version.

Here are the first four bars of a simple-melody circle of fifths version. Try to complete it. Compare how it sounds to the original version.

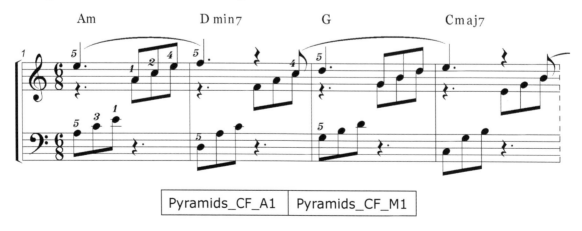

| Pyramids_CF_A1 | Pyramids_CF_M1 |

The Pyramids circle of fifths chord sequence

Of course, if we change the bottom note of a left hand Pyramids chord, we will have changed the root, and therefore the chord will have a new name.

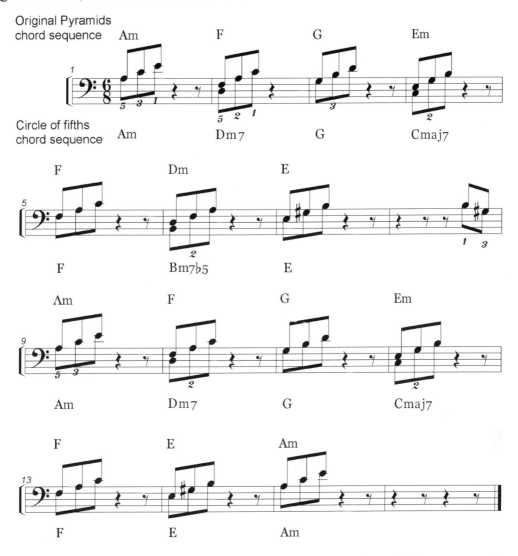

These new chords are called seventh chords. There are keyboard diagrams on the next page.

Here are all the seventh chords in the Pyramids circle of fifths version. The shaded diamond marks the old root.

Dmin7 (bars 2 and 10)

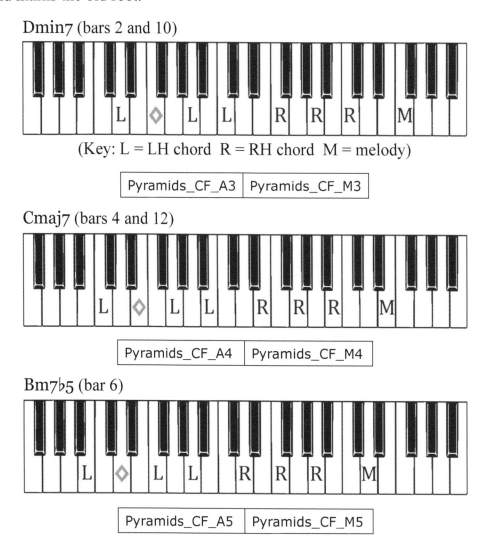

(Key: L = LH chord   R = RH chord   M = melody)

| Pyramids_CF_A3 | Pyramids_CF_M3 |

Cmaj7 (bars 4 and 12)

| Pyramids_CF_A4 | Pyramids_CF_M4 |

Bm7♭5 (bar 6)

| Pyramids_CF_A5 | Pyramids_CF_M5 |

You already know minor seventh chords. The Bm7♭5 ('B minor seven flat five') is the only new type of chord here. It looks like a D minor chord with B as a bass note.

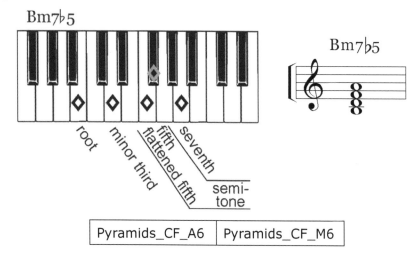

| Pyramids_CF_A6 | Pyramids_CF_M6 |

126

Previous versions of Pyramids and the circle of fifths

It's easy to over-use the circle of fifths. For practice, play the Pyramids version on the next page, which uses all the possible circle of fifths chords. Then play the versions shown in the chord charts on this page, which use only some of the possible circle of fifths chords. In a way, versions with fewer circle of fifths chords sound more sophisticated than ones that use every possible circle of fifths chord.

	1 original chords						(LH-over pattern)	
A¹	Am	F	G	Em	F	Dm	E	E

	9 two substituted circle of fifths chords						(LH-over pattern)	
A²	Am	Dm7	G	Cmaj7	F	E	Am	Am

Pyramids_CF_A7	Pyramids_CF_M7

A 32-bar AABA version incorporating the circle of fifths might look like this:

	1 original chords						(LH-over pattern)	
A¹	Am	F	G	Em	F	Dm	E	E

	9 two substituted circle of fifths chords						(LH-over pattern)	
A¹	Am	F	G	Cmaj7	F	Bm7♭5	E	E

	17 chords do not change						(LH-over pattern)	
B	Fmaj7	G	Em7	Am	F	D♯dim7	E	E

	25 two substituted circle of fifths chords						(LH-over ending)	
A²	Am	Dm7	G	Cmaj7	F	E ↗	Am	Am

Pyramids_CF_A8	Pyramids_CF_M8

127

Pyramids A¹A² with Circle of Fifths Chords

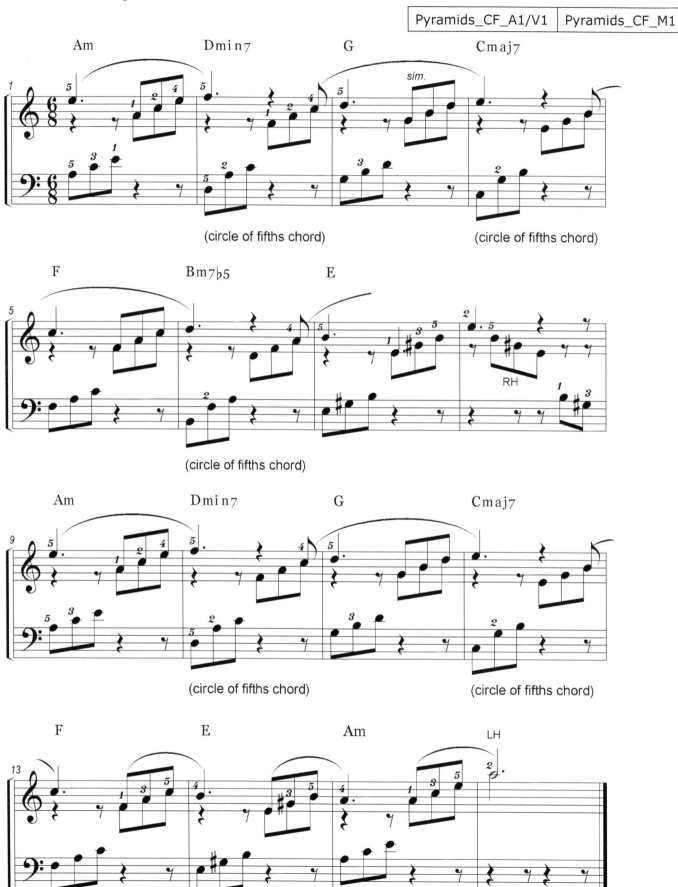

Suspensions

| AUDIO 4 | MIDI 2 | Lesson performance: | Pyramids_SUS_A1/V1 | Pyramids_SUS_M1 |

Suspensions are an easy way to get more out of chords.

A suspension is the temporary raising by one scale step of a chord tone. Releasing the note back into its proper position is called 'resolving' the suspension, or its 'resolution'. Suspensions are indicated in chord symbols by 'sus' for the suspension and 'res' for the resolution (optional).

Here are some simple G and E suspended and resolved chords:

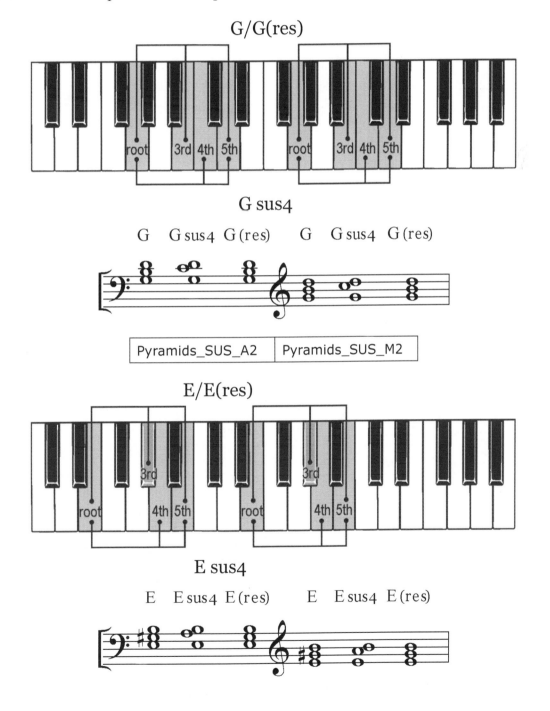

G/G(res)

G sus4

G   G sus4   G (res)   G   G sus4   G (res)

| Pyramids_SUS_A2 | Pyramids_SUS_M2 |

E/E(res)

E sus4

E   E sus4   E (res)   E   E sus4   E (res)

The root, third or fifth of a chord can be suspended and then resolved (raised and then lowered). These are the bottom, middle and top notes of a root position (BMP) triad. But the third – the middle note of a BMP chord or root position triad – is the note which is most often 'suspended'. It is pulled up into the fourth step above the root. The Pyramids material puts 'sus4' to help you see that it is the third that has been raised a step to the fourth. Usually you would just see 'sus' which on its own means 'raise the third of this chord a step to the fourth'.

The Pyramids book also puts 'res' at the place the fourth falls back to its home position – another helpful reminder you won't usually find in sheet music. Usually you would just see the chord symbol repeated, but without the 'sus', and that is how you would know to let the suspended note fall back.

You need quite a bit of time on one chord for a suspension/resolution pair. The obvious place in Pyramids to use the suspension/resolution option is the two bars of chord E (bars 7 and 8 of the 16-bar A^1A^2 version).

Here are some examples:

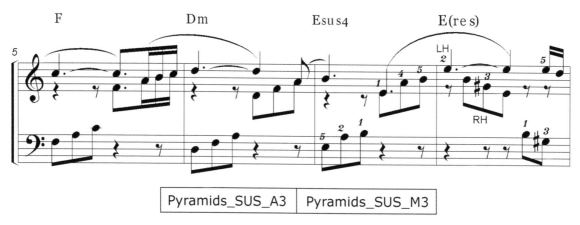

Pyramids_SUS_A3 | Pyramids_SUS_M3

The Esus4 chords in the third bar of this line of music are shown in the keyboard diagrams on page 129.

Here is the same technique applied to the Descending Variations:

Here is the same suspension/resolution technique in the four-four 3+3+2 pattern:

In this case, the Esus4 chord resolves to a first inversion chord – but the suspended fourth stills falls back to the third according to plan.

Pavane in the Circle of Fifths with suspensions

The next piece of music is a slow Pyramids variation with plenty of time for suspensions and resolutions. (A pavane is a slow dance.) As well as the three-note suspensions and resolutions shown above, the Pavane uses seventh chords with suspended fourths. You can see that the bottom three notes do exactly the same as in the diagrams on page 129 – the chords just have an added seventh.

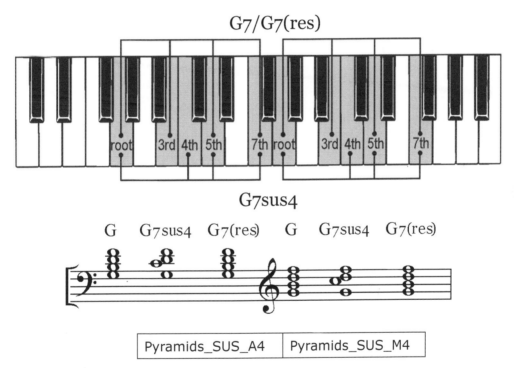

| Pyramids_SUS_A4 | Pyramids_SUS_M4 |

(The E7(sus) chord is diagrammed after the music, on page 134.)

Pavane: Pyramids with Circle of Fifths Chords and Suspensions

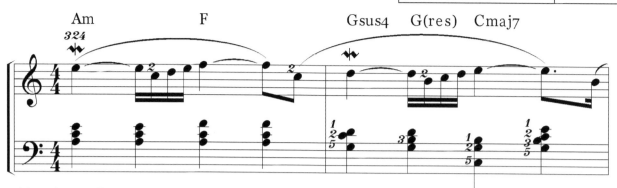

(At a slow walking pace. With the pedal.)

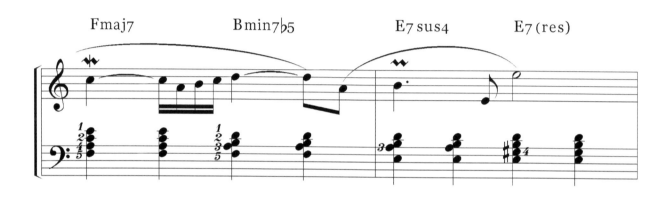

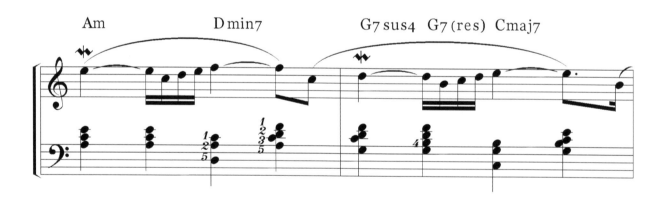

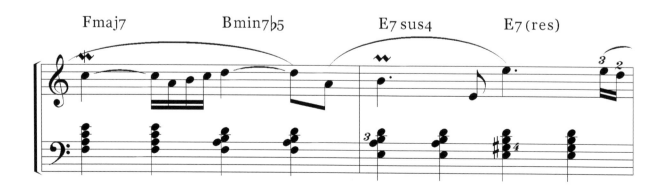

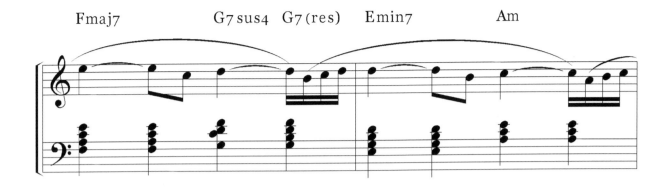

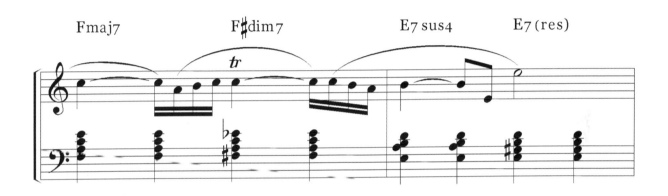

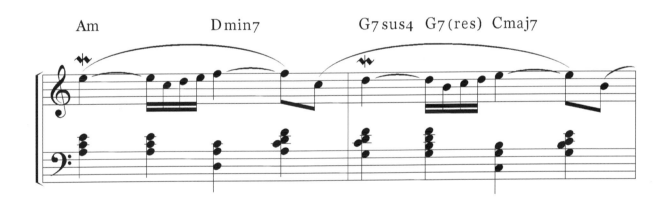

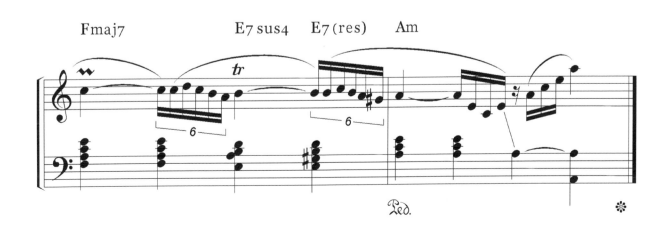

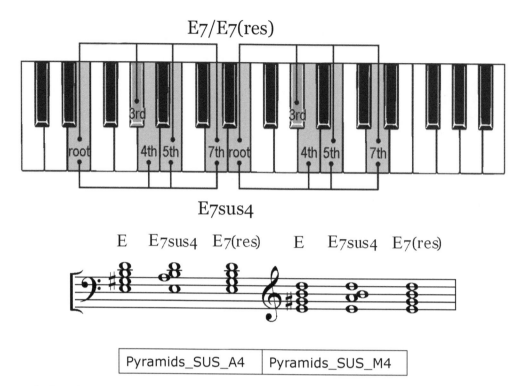

Pyramids_SUS_A4	Pyramids_SUS_M4

The usual chord symbols would be 'G7sus' and plain 'G7' (for example), but the music here gives you the helpful extra 'res' indication, as before.

The 'Suspensions and syncopation in four-four' variation in the final Further Variations section uses suspensions as often as possible. In bar 6, look out for a Dmin sus2 chord, where the root is the note pulled up then released.

Also note that all the suspensions in the Pyramids volume are what are called 'unprepared suspensions' – that is, they are played without the normal ('un-suspended', or 'res') chord being played first.

Further Variations

| AUDIO 4 | MIDI 2 | Performances: | Pyramids_FV_A1–8 | Pyramids_FV_M1-8 |
| | | | (FV_V1–8) | |

This volume has shown throughout how elements like the melody line, the bass line, the triad-based accompaniment and the rhythm can be varied and combined to create new versions of Pyramids. The additional variations in this section show some more possibilities.

Method

Starting an accompaniment pattern and keeping it going all the way through a chord sequence is a valuable part of the accomplished keyboard player's skills. Note that instant improvised arrangements aren't being suggested, but rather working arrangements up over time, perhaps modifying ideas in whole or in part according to the possibilities and limitations and what 'sounds right'.

A teacher working with a more advanced pupil (or a mature student working alone) could study just the first line of any of the variations in this section, work out what pattern they are built on, and try to complete the variation by playing the rest of the chord sequence in that pattern.

Variation: Mixed inversions in six-eight

| Pyramids_FV_A1/V1 | Pyramids_FV_M1 |

This relatively simple variation could be offered as a supplement to the Mixed Inversions module on page 105. It is ideally suited to the 'method' described at the start of this section and to a simple bass-line 'circle of fifths' treatment.

Variation: Melody over rising and falling inversions

| Pyramids_FV_A2/V2 | Pyramids_FV_M2 |

This variation has already been presented on page 109, but is here written out on three staves.

This way of presenting the variation shows more obviously how the melody is added onto the accompaniment pattern. It also models the skill of the keyboard player who is meeting the challenge of playing a melody while keeping a rhythmic accompaniment with a regular pattern going. Playing from this arrangement is useful even if the pupil has already played the previous version.

Variation: Developed melody with developed bass line

| Pyramids_FV_A3/V3 | Pyramids_FV_M3 |

This variation adds the developed bass line to the six-eight developed melody version on page 43 and could be offered as a continuation of the module Developing the Bass Line, starting on page 83. Only the two extra bass line approach notes in each bar are new.

Variation: Melody in the left hand

Pyramids_FV_A4/V4	Pyramids_FV_M4

Playing the melody in the left hand is an obvious way of getting more out of familiar material. The pupil will benefit from painstaking counting and together, left, right (TLR) analysis (see page 117). See the 'Mixed inversions in four-four with syncopation' variation in on page 145 for a fully worked-out example.

Variation: Melody plus LH-over patterns plus developed bass line

Pyramids_FV_A5/V5	Pyramids_FV_M5

This variation combines the developed melody with 12-note left-hand-over patterns and the developed bass line and continues the theme of the previous variation. The melody sits inside the LH-over patterns, which run both below and above it. The variation is shown on three staves; the task is to play all three lines of music at once. The stems-down developed bass line can be left out initially if desired.

Variation: Melody over falling-then-rising inversions

Pyramids_FV_A6/V6	Pyramids_FV_M6

The theme is continued in this variation, which combines the melody and a new accompaniment pattern consisting of falling then rising triads, incorporating second inversion triads for the first time. Both the left and right hand triads are shown on the lower stave, the right hand stems up and the left stems down. Note that the fingering given is for rehearsing the falling-then-rising inversions, and has to be changed to incorporate the melody.

Variation: Mixed inversions in four-four with syncopation

Pyramids_FV_A7/V7	Pyramids_FV_M7

This variation shows how material in the more classical six eight rhythm can be adapted into the 'rockier' four-four rhythm, particularly for younger players. The rhythm of the left hand is a rock staple. Together, left, right analysis will help the pupil. Pay particular attention to the instruction on page 118 to let yourself abandon the rhythm temporarily while drilling the TLR 'sequence of events'.

Variation: Suspensions and syncopation in four-four

Pyramids_FV_A8/V8	Pyramids_FV_M8

This variation is again set out in a way which models a creative keyboard player's thought processes and skills. The variation is presented in skeletal form, as it exists in the player's mind, first. The first line of the 'realisation' (the playing-out of the structure) is very simple, but developments of the melodic line created by the suspensions and resolutions soon follow. Count the left hand rhythms carefully.

Variation: Mixed inversions in six-eight

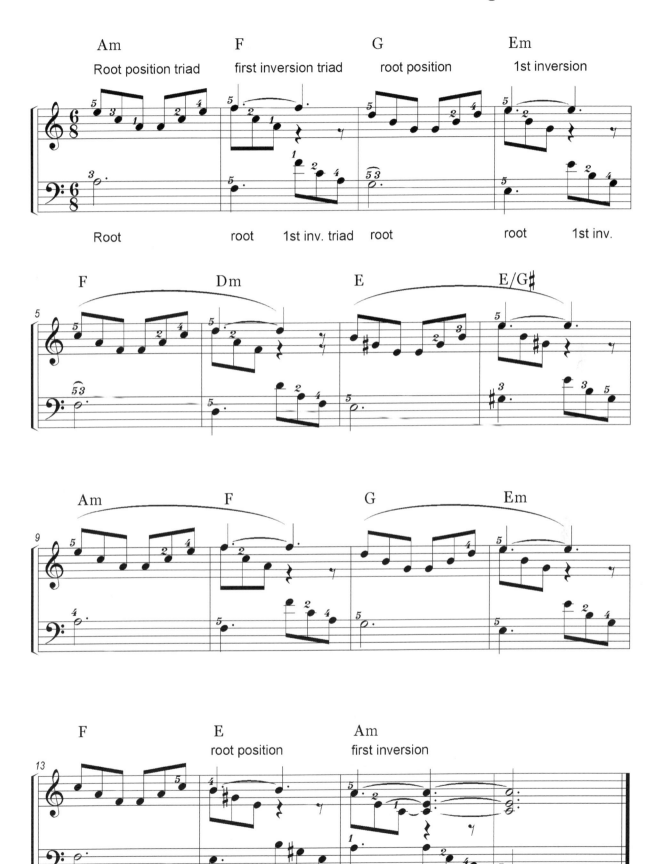

Variation: Melody over rising and falling inversions

Variation: Developed melody and developed bass line

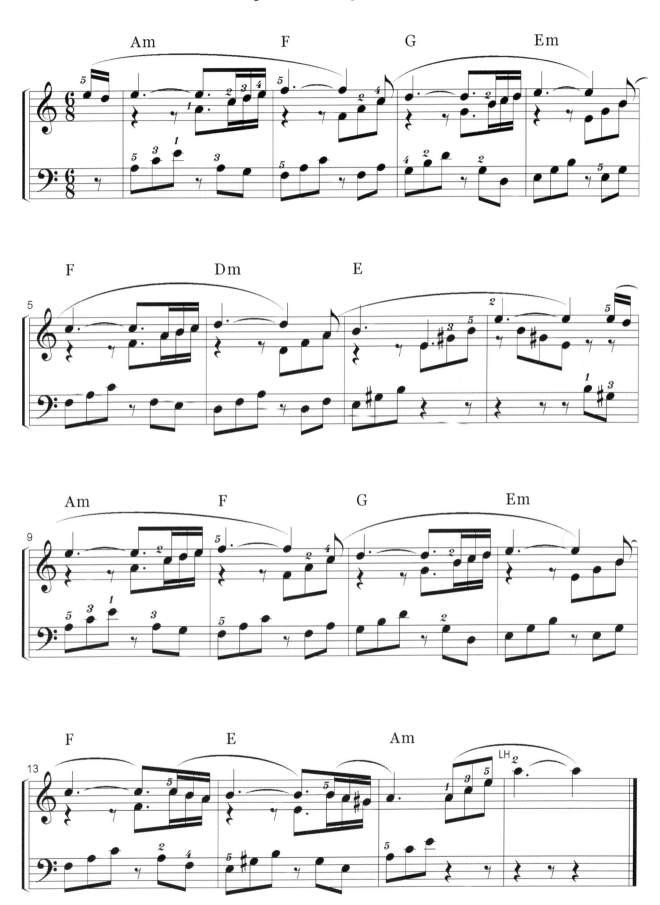

Variation: Melody in the left hand

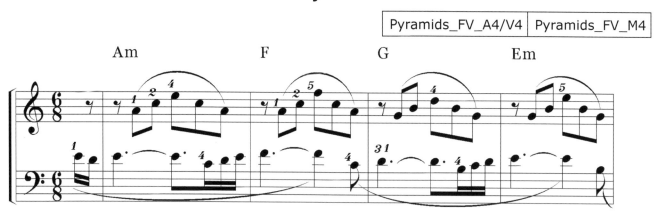

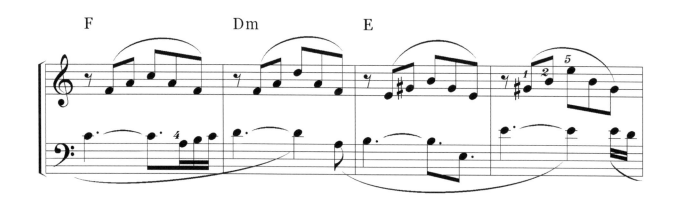

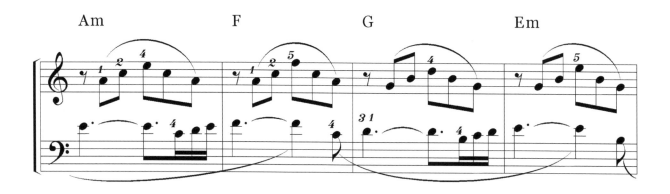

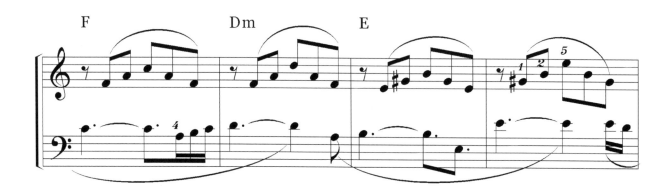

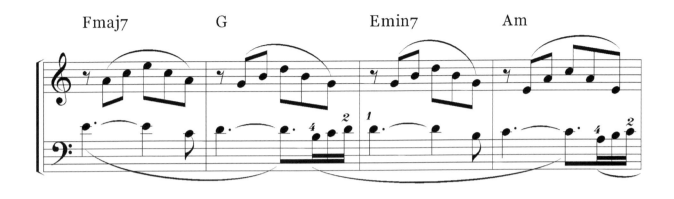

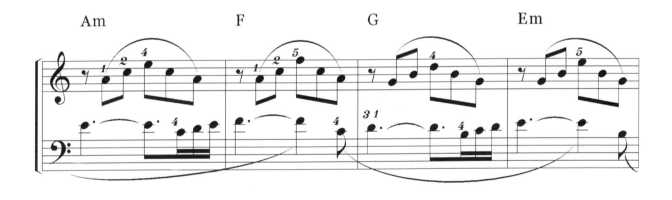

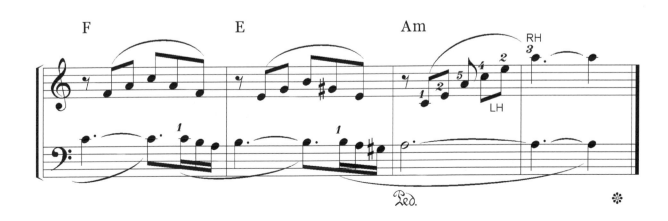

Variation: Melody plus LH-over patterns plus developed bass line

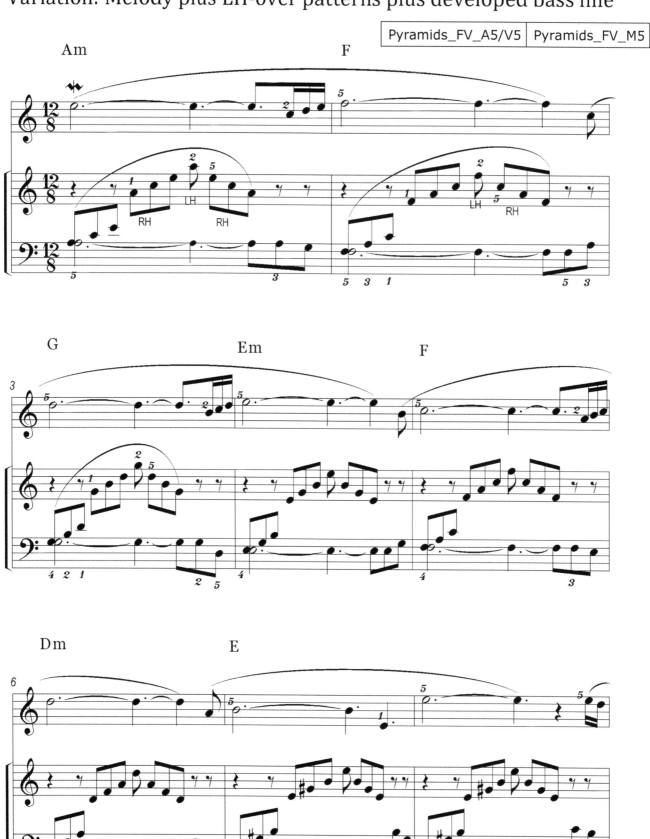

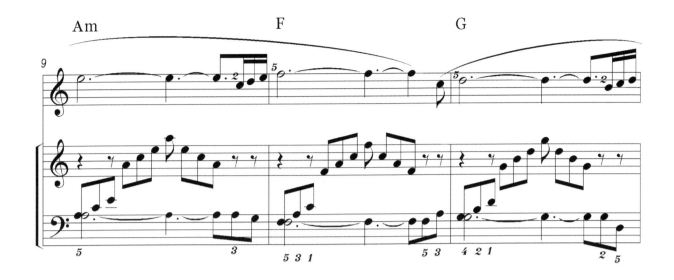

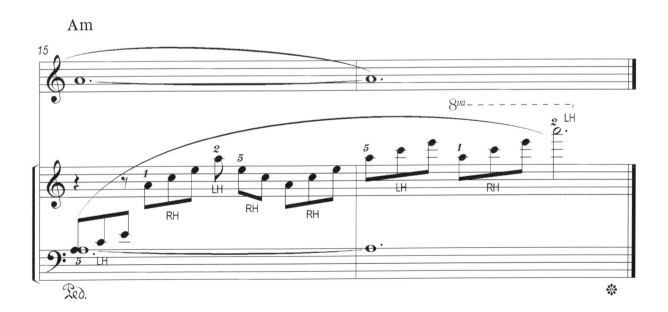

Variation: Melody over falling-then-rising inversions

Second inversion   root position   2nd inv.   root pos.

2nd inv.   2nd inv.   1st inv.

Note: The fingering given is for rehearsing the inversions, which should be learnt separately first.
The fingering has to be changed slightly to incorporate the melody.

Variation: Mixed inversions in four-four with syncopation

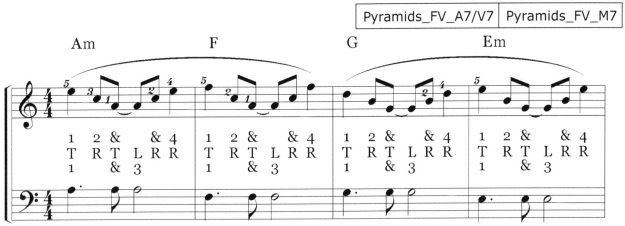

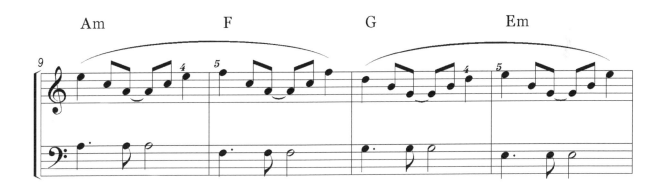

Variation: Suspensions and syncopation in four-four

Postscript to the Pyramids Variations

The many 'realisations' of the Pyramids chord sequence explored in this volume by no means exhaust the possibilities. Committed students will find many more if they give themselves over to their own creativity and 'just sit down and play'.

Here are some suggestions.

- The Pyramids material can be treated freely as regards 'form'. Different structures, such as a possible $A^1 A^2 B A^1 A^2$ version, can be tried out. The extended endings heard in popular song, can be tried, repeating the F/E pair of chords in bars 13/14 of an $A^1 A^2$ version, or the comparable pair in a 32-bar version. For performance, prolonged medleys of variations can be put together, with transitional phrases between, or even modulations into other keys.

- Melodic variation has not been explored in the present volume. The musician can play a (two-hand) accompaniment texture and listen internally for a different melody which fits with the Pyramids chord sequence, and then pick out his or her idea at the keyboard.

- Once they are able to maintain an accompaniment pattern, students can create other A minor chord sequences using the Pyramids chords.

- The rhythms and textures which the Pyramids chord sequence can support are, of course, endless. There are chord textures in this volume which have been only partially explored and other time signatures – such as three-four – which have not been examined at all.

- Visit the Pyramids sections of the Musicarta website and YouTube channels for more developmental material, such as the three 'seed versions' deliberately left incomplete for pupils to finish. A committed composition or improvisation teacher can easily provide similar examples.

- The Pyramids melody (with or without variations and improvisations) can be played by a solo instrument with free keyboard accompaniment. Two keyboard players who know the material can work up keyboard duet arrangements. The material could even be performed by a rock combo.

- Where two keyboards are available, multiple four-hand possibilities arise, with the teacher or senior player playing a duet part or providing a background accompaniment to the pupil's practising and soloing.

- Once known, the Pyramids chord sequence can be the focus of intensive ear training, either 'freestyle' or in line with exam syllabi. In a two-keyboard teaching situation, copying melodic fragments and textures in a call-and-response texture is particularly fruitful.

Moving forward, it is hoped that students of the Pyramids Variations will exploit the potential of having explored the Pyramids chord sequence so well by applying the skills learnt to other material, and use the Pyramids Variations as a springboard into their own creative futures.

About Musicarta

Musicarta Publications and the musicarta.com website are committed to helping keyboard players of all ages and stages develop their creative keyboard skills.

Musicarta offers three major home study courses.

The Pyramids Variations has shown you how to play a chord sequence and develop a basic keyboard pattern into an endless variety of pieces. The Pyramids Variations is Musicarta's simplest introduction to keyboard creativity.

The Canon Project uses the same combination of text, illustrations and audio-visual learning support material to teach you to improvise on this timeless and much-loved chord sequence – itself the basis for numerous popular music hits.

Musicarta Key Chords Vol.1 is a fast-track approach to learning popular music harmony, and develops your chord vocabulary by teaching the four chords you're most likely to find together in music, in attractive rhythmic keyboard riffs.

Key Chords focuses particularly on the build-up of syncopated keyboard textures. Both Key Chords and the Canon Project introduce transposing – the ability to play chord sequences in a number of different keys.

All three courses are available as digital downloads via the website and have content-rich sampler pages on the site so you can choose the course which best suits you. Downloads consist of an illustration-rich PDF file with audio and MIDI files for all the musical examples, a Windows OS desktop 'virtual keyboard' MIDI file player, and either include teaching videos or access to restricted videos online.

The three projects offer an ideal 'creative' supplement to traditional exam-syllabus piano lessons, and Musicarta's media-rich learning material means anyone can make good progress without being able to read music particularly well. Musicarta Key Chords Vol.1 is available as a Kindle book, and Key Chords and the Canon Project are scheduled for Amazon print-on-demand publication before 2013 year-end.

The 'Mister Musicarta' YouTube channel hosts project videos which keep these projects alive with 'diary entry' ideas to inspire your continuing explorations. The Musicarta YouTube channel also showcases the Musicarta 'Solos' series – a perfect opportunity to train your fingers in the popular music solo keyboard style.

Musicarta on YouTube offers an ever-increasing number of music theory video lessons, while the www.musicarta.com website has nearly 200 pages dedicated to de-mystifying music theory, making your practising more effective and putting pop music keyboard styles at your fingertips.

Visit www.musicarta.com, take the tour, and let
Musicarta become your creative keyboard companion!

Printed in Great Britain
by Amazon.co.uk, Ltd.,
Marston Gate.